man's psychic life: elements and structures

Cover illustration: a crystal

Omraam Mikhaël Aïvanhov

man's psychic life: elements and structures

Translated from the French

Collection Izvor
No. 222

EDITIONS PROSVETA

By the same author:
(translated from the French)

Izvor Collection

Prosveta S.A. – B.P. 12 – 83601 Fréjus Cedex (France)

ISBN 2-85566-389-X
édition originale : 2-85566-368-7

TABLE OF CONTENTS

The reader will better understand certain aspects of the lectures published in the present volume, if he bears in mind that Master's Omraam Mikhaël Aïvanhov's Teaching is exclusively oral.

1

KNOW THYSELF

Very few people have ever correctly interpreted the ancient precept inscribed over the entrance to the sanctuary at Delphi: 'Know Thyself'. Who is this 'thyself' whom we must know? Is it a question of getting to know our own character with all its weaknesses, faults and qualities? No; if to 'know oneself' were nothing more than that, the Sages of old would never have caused the precept to be carved over the door of a temple. It is necessary, to be sure, to know one's own character, but it is not enough: to know oneself is much more than that. To know oneself is to become conscious of the different bodies of which we are composed, from the subtlest to the most opaque, to be conscious of the principles which inform them, of the needs we experience because of them and of the states of consciousness which correspond to each one. But men know nothing of these things. Everybody glances into himself from time to time and learns to recognize his principal strengths and weaknesses, and then he says, 'Oh, I know myself!' But he is wrong: he does not know himself yet.

The fact is that there is no one theory of man which fully accounts for his extreme complexity, and it should not surprise us to learn that the different religions and philosophical schools of thought have all had different notions of the structure of man. Hindus, for instance, consider that a human being is made up of seven component parts, and the Theosophists have adopted the same system. Astrology divides man into twelve parts, corresponding to the twelve signs of the Zodiac, whereas Alchemy divides him into four, corresponding to the four elements. Cabbalists see four or ten components in man, corresponding to the four worlds or the ten Sephiroth. In ancient Persia, Mazdaism and Manichaeism divided man into two, corresponding to the two Principles of Good and Evil, Light and Darkness, Ormuzd and Ahriman. As for the Christians, they often divide man into three: body, soul and spirit. And, finally, I should add that certain esoterics divide man into nine component parts, because nine represents the Three in the three worlds: physical, spiritual and divine.

So which system possesses the truth? All of them. It just depends on one's point of view. We cannot reject any of them. Personally, for the sake of convenience, I often divide man into two parts: the lower nature or personality and the higher nature or individuality, because this division makes it easier to understand certain problems. In other instances, if I think it will help to make things clearer to you, I may speak of the three, six or seven components of man. These systems of division are, after all, simply a convenient way of understanding one or other aspect of the whole. None of them contradicts the others because each one is true from its own point of view.

When an anatomist wants to give a clear and comprehensible picture of human anatomy, instead of trying to put everything onto one diagram, he presents a series of superimposed plates or diagrams illustrating the different physiological systems: skeleton, muscles and nerves, blood vessels, etc. Geographers use the same technique: a series of different maps indicating the physical, political, economic and geological realities of the planet. The same system can be applied in different domains and, like the anatomist or the geographer, an Initiate uses different charts or outlines according to the particular aspects of man or the particular question he wants to study.

2

THE SYNOPTIC TABLE

'That which is below is like to that which is above, and that which is above is like to that which is below', said Hermes Trismegistus. The existence within man, of certain subtle principles, each of which has its own needs and activities, can be readily understood if one takes the needs and activities of the physical body as a starting point. This is what I want to show you with the help of this synoptic table (Figure 1), in which I have attempted to combine all the principal elements of our physical and psychic life.

Let's begin with the physical body: what are its needs? First and foremost it needs health. In order to be healthy it has to eat, so it needs food. But then it must have money in order to buy food and it cannot have money unless it works for it. You see? It is simple! And now, since what is below on the physical level, is like that which is above on the spiritual level, it stands to reason that we shall find exactly the same pattern at work on the other, subtler levels, in connection with man's other, subtler principles: his will, heart, mind, soul and spirit. Each of these principles has its own particular goal; in order to attain its goal it needs nourishment; in order to obtain that nourishment it needs money, and it can only earn the money it needs by doing a particular type of work.

Take the case of the will: the goal of the will is movement and power. It needs to act on other objects, beings and situations in order to shape and transform them. But in order to be active the will needs nourishment, and its nourishment is force. Only if the will is nourished by force can it manifest itself, and in order to purchase the force it needs, the will needs money, and its money is the physical gesture. If you want to set your energies in motion you have to begin by freeing yourself from the grip of inertia and immobility. When the will acquires the habit of acting, of moving, of doing, it purchases force and becomes strong and powerful. Every physical effort you make helps to strengthen your will.

Next we come to the heart. What does the heart need? It needs to feel itself expanding with warmth, joy and happiness. The food of the heart is feelings and the currency it uses to purchase that food is love. When you love, your love is 'money' which enables you to 'buy', that is to say, to experience, all kinds of feelings, sensations and emotions. If you lose your love you lose all that warmth and happiness; you find yourself out in the cold. How can you keep the wealth that your love has earned you? By cultivating harmony in your relations with the universe and all its creatures.

And the intellect, the mind, what is it looking for? The intellect needs to be illuminated, it seeks light, knowledge. The food of the intellect is thought. The money with which it can buy the best food is wisdom, and the activity by which the intellect earns wisdom is meditation. Only wisdom is capable of nourishing your mind with the very best thoughts so that it can obtain the light it seeks.

The ideal of the soul is space, immensity. The human soul is a tiny particle of the Universal Soul and it feels so constricted and hemmed in within man that its one desire is to be allowed to expand in limitless space. In order to attain this goal the soul, too, needs nourishment to keep up its strength, and the particular type of food which suits it best is all the qualities and virtues of the higher consciousness: impersonality, abnegation and self-sacrifice. The coin with which it buys this food is ecstasy, fusion with the divine world, and the work which enables it to earn this fusion is the

PRINCIPLE	IDEAL	NOURISHMENT	PRICE	ACTIVITY
SPIRIT	ETERNITY	FREEDOM	TRUTH	IDENTIFICATION
SOUL	THE INFINITE	IMPERSONALITY	ECSTASY	CONTEMPLATION ADORATION PRAYER
INTELLECT	KNOWLEDGE LEARNING LIGHT	THOUGHTS	WISDOM	MEDITATION
HEART	HAPPINESS WARMTH	FEELINGS	LOVE	HARMONIOUS AND ARTISTIC ACTIVITIES
WILL	POWER MOVEMENT	FORCE	GESTURE BREATH	BREATHING GYMNASTICS
PHYSICAL BODY	HEALTH LIFE	FOOD	MONEY	PHYSICAL WORK

Figure 1 – The synoptic table

work of prayer and contemplation. Yes, the specific activity of the soul is contemplation.

The ideal of the spirit is eternity, for the essence of the spirit is immortal; it transcends time. But in order to attain eternity, the spirit, too, needs food and the food of the spirit is freedom. The soul needs to expand in space and the spirit needs to break its bonds and free itself. Truth is the coin with which the spirit purchases freedom. Every truth, about anything whatever, is liberating. Jesus said, 'Know the truth and the truth will set you free.' Yes, it is truth which sets us free and the activity which puts us in possession of truth is identification with the Creator. He who identifies with the Creator becomes one with Him, possesses the truth and is free! When Jesus said, 'My Father and I are one', he summed up in those few words this whole process of identification.

In this table I have tried to put together a unified, coordinated picture of the principal elements of our physical and, especially, of our psychic life which are usually scattered and disconnected, and these notions could, of course, be developed and detailed almost indefinitely. The table does not contain everything, of course; there are a certain number of notions that you will not find in it, but you can, at least, see where the different levels or degrees of consciousness fit in: the unconscious, the subconscious, consciousness, self-consciousness and the super-conscious.

A great many philosophers, psychologists and psychoanalysts have studied this question of the different levels of human consciousness. Their findings are very interesting but it is often difficult to see exactly how they relate to one's everyday experience, so let me give you a simple example which you will easily understand. Suppose that you have a bad fall and hit your head so hard that you are knocked unconscious. If someone gives you first aid you will begin to stir, but your eyes remain closed: this is a state of subconsciousness. After a little while you open your eyes and realize that you are lying on the ground, that there are people round you, but you still have no idea of what has happened to you: this is the state of consciousness. Before long you are back to normal: you can feel pain and you remember what happened to you and how it happened: this is the state of self-consciousness. And finally, when you have completely recovered, you can feel joy and gratitude to Heaven for having been protected, for it could have been so much worse. This is the state of superconsciousness. I think that should be perfectly clear to you now.

And now let us see how the different elements which constitute our being correspond to these different levels of consciousness. The physical body itself corresponds to the unconscious. The manifestations of physiological life (breathing, digestion, circulation of the blood, elimination, growth, etc.) correspond to the subconscious. That which concerns the will and the heart corresponds to the level of consciousness, whereas self-consciousness begins only on the level of the intellect. Finally, superconsciousness corresponds to that which concerns the soul and the spirit; in fact one could say that the domain of the spirit corresponds to the divine superconsciousness.

But to revert to the essential purpose of this table: it shows clearly how to work with all the different principles within you without neglecting any one of them. Only those who learn how to work every day with their physical body, their will, heart, mind, soul and spirit, will one day reach perfect fulfilment.

3

SEVERAL SOULS AND SEVERAL BODIES

All the great Initiates, who have an intimate and exact understanding of human nature thanks to their clairvoyance, agree that the soul, that animating principle which indwells a human being's physical body, is not given to a child in its entirety at the moment of birth. It enters into him progressively, in successive stages throughout his life.

It is not surprising, therefore, that Neoplatonic philosophers and even some of the early Fathers of the Church held that man possessed several different souls. The first of these, the *vital soul,* is purely vegetative; it controls the physiological functions of breathing, nutrition, circulation, etc. The second is more highly evolved and is known as the *animal soul;* the third is the *sensitive* or emotional soul; the fourth is known as the *rational* or reasonable soul, and, finally, there is

the *divine soul,* the soul of pure light which is possessed only by Initiates who have completed their
evolution.

The most basic, the vegetative soul, enters
and animates the embryo while it is still in the
womb. At the age of seven a child receives its
animal or voluntary soul. The belief that at this
age, the 'age of reason', a child enters into full possession of his soul, is a very common error. No,
the fact is that the soul it receives is still only the
voluntary or animal soul. From the time it is
born, a child is constantly in motion, moving his
arms and legs, walking and running and jumping
about, and by the time he is seven and his animal
soul has fully entered his body you could say that
he has acquired sufficient physical autonomy to
be in control of his movements.

For some time before this, however, a new
phase has already begun, the phase during which
the affective dimension becomes gradually more
important: it is the sensitive or emotional soul
which has begun to develop. At about fourteen,
when a child reaches puberty, the sensitive soul
reaches maturity and enters fully into him, lead-
ing him to give priority to his emotions.

At the same time the capacity for reflection
begins to develop and, at the age of twenty-one, it
is the intellectual or rational soul which enters
fully into a human being. This does not mean that

a person automatically becomes wise and reasonable at the age of twenty-one. Far from it! In fact it is at this age that he is capable of making the biggest mistakes of his life! But it is at this age that he takes full possession of his powers of comprehension and reasoning.

As for the divine soul, its coming depends entirely on the kind of life we have chosen to live and on our desire to receive it. Initiation is just that, the path a human being treads in order to seek out his divine soul and persuade it to take up permanent residence in him. An Initiate is one who has worked to transform his whole being so as to draw his divine soul into himself; his whole being vibrates in harmony, in unison with Cosmic Intelligence, for he has become Its servant and conductor.

In fact, though, only a few very exceptional beings who have spent many incarnations working for this goal actually achieve it. Their one idea has always been to fulfil themselves and attract their divine soul to themselves so as to be able to manifest themselves in all their plenitude. For years and years, by means of their spiritual exercises of purification, meditation, prayer and sacrifice, they have prepared themselves to attract and become one with their higher Self, their divine Self. And when they attain their goal we say that they have received the Holy Spirit.

The Cabbalists also teach that man has several souls. The emotional or astral soul known as Nephesh; the intellectual or rational soul, Ruah, and the three higher souls: Neshamah, Haia and Yehida. The Hindus, on the other hand, speak of bodies rather than souls and this is equally correct, for every particle of matter contains its own energy. This energy is the masculine principle and the matter is the feminine principle. Everywhere, on every level of the universe, matter contains energy and man's material, physical body possesses its own specific energy. It is this energy which we call the soul. But above and beyond his physical body, man has other, subtler bodies and each one of these subtle bodies possesses its own soul. The vital soul belongs to the physical body; the emotional or sensitive soul belongs to the astral body; the intellectual or rational soul belongs to the mental body, and the three higher bodies, causal, buddhic and atmic, possess three higher souls. Each body, therefore, contains its soul: the body is the form or container and the soul is the energy which animates it. The two cannot be separated. Nature itself, the cosmos as a whole, is a body, God's body, and its soul is the Universal Soul. All this is perfectly clear.

But let us get back to the different bodies of man. The three fundamental activities characteristic of man are thought (by means of the intellect or mind), feelings (by means of the heart) and action (by means of the physical body). You must not think that only the physical body is material; the heart and mind are also material instruments but the matter of which they are made is far subtler than that of the physical body.

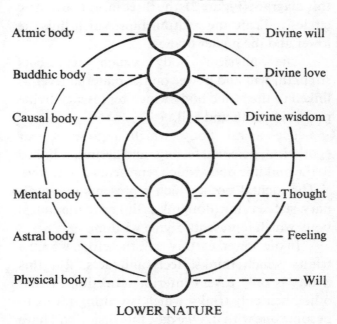

Figure 2 – The two trinities of man's higher and lower natures

An age-old esoteric tradition teaches that the support or vehicle of feeling is the astral body and that of the intellect, the mental body. But this trinity made up of our physical, astral and mental bodies, constitutes our imperfect human nature, and the three faculties of thought, feeling and action also exist on a higher level, their vehicles being, respectively, the causal, buddhic and atmic bodies which go to make up our divine Self. In this diagram (Figure 2), the three large concentric circles indicate the relationships which link the lower and the higher bodies.

The physical body which represents strength, will and power on the material level, is linked to the atmic body which represents divine power, strength and will.

The astral body which represents our egotistical, personal feelings and desires, is linked to the buddhic body which represents divine love.

The mental body which represents our ordinary, self-serving thoughts, is linked to the causal body which represents divine wisdom.

In our lower, earthly self, therefore, we are a trinity which thinks, feels and acts. But this trinity is only a very inferior reflection of that other, heavenly trinity which is waiting for us to become one with it. One day, this fusion will have to take place. That is the deep, hidden meaning of the mystic symbol which is known as Solomon's

Seal ✡ , but which existed long before Solomon. Initiates often sum up a very profound spiritual or psychic reality in a symbol or a simple geometrical figure.

A human being, therefore, is made up of three bodies (or, if you prefer, three souls) which constitute his lower self and which are destined, one day, to unite with the three bodies (or souls) which constitute his higher Self. Every experience in life, whether it be happy or unhappy, exists for this one purpose: to enable us to find and become one with our true Selves. When our lower self melts into our higher Self and forms one, then all Heaven and earth are united within us in fullness, abundance and joy.

4

HEART, MIND, SOUL AND SPIRIT

One of the best known passages in the Gospels is the one in which a scribe asked Jesus which was the first commandment of all, and Jesus replied, 'The first of all the commandments is... You shall love the Lord your God with all your heart, with all your soul, with all your mind, and with all your strength.' By these words Jesus indicated that man was composed of these four principles: heart, mind, soul and spirit. The word 'strength' designates the spirit for, according to Initiatic Science, only the spirit possesses true force or strength.

If we are to understand the full import of these words, we have to begin by establishing a clear distinction between the heart and the soul on the one hand, and the intellect or mind and the spirit on the other. The heart and the soul are both vehicles of our emotions, feelings and desires but whereas the heart is the seat of our ordinary, earthly emotions stemming from our sensuality and from the torments and disappointments of life or from purely physical pleasures and joys, the soul is the seat of our divine, spiritual emotions and impulses. The same sort of distinction must be made between the mind and the spirit: the mind is the seat of our ordinary, everyday thoughts and reasoning which concern only the satisfaction of our personal interests and our most material needs, whereas the spirit, on the contrary, is the seat of purely disinterested thoughts and activity.

The heart and the soul are both related to the one, feminine principle which manifests itself either on the lower level of the heart or astral plane, or on the higher level of the soul or buddhic plane. Similarly, the mind and the spirit both stem from the masculine principle which can also manifest itself on the lower, mental level or on the higher, causal level. The two principles, therefore, masculine and feminine, each use two different vehicles: the heart, the mind, the soul and the spirit. And the two principles dwell together with the four vehicles in one and the same 'house': our physical body.

I realize that all this is still rather abstract and difficult for some of you, so I shall try to make it a little clearer by illustrating it with a story. Picture to yourself a house in which there is a master and a mistress with a man-servant and a maid. Every now and then the master of the house has to go away on a business trip and his wife stays to look after things at home, feeling a bit listless and lonely while she waits for her husband to come home again. And when he does come, loaded with all kinds of presents, everything is joy and light again. But then it also happens that the master and mistress go off together, and when that happens the maid and the man-servant, finding themselves free and with no one to keep an eye on them, decide to make the most of their freedom and begin to explore all the private cupboards and closets. There, they discover food and drink and, on the principle of 'the more the merrier' they invite their friends in for a party. Well, after a few hours of feasting and merrymaking, bottles have been spilled, tables have been overturned and a few skulls have been cracked. A truly horrifying spectacle greets the master and mistress when they get home and, naturally, they reprimand the servants and order them to clean up everything and restore order.

And now let's interpret this little story. The house is the physical body; the maid is the heart, the man-servant is the mind; the mistress of the house is the soul and the master is the spirit. The spirit often leaves us and when it is away the soul is lonely and feels abandoned. But when the spirit comes home again it brings with it an abundance of inspiration and light. When the soul and spirit leave home together, then the heart and mind can't wait to commit every possible kind of folly in the company of other foolish hearts and minds!

And now, if we look at this story a little more closely, we shall see many details about the respective roles of the heart, mind, soul and spirit. As you know, a maid usually attends to the needs of her mistress, whereas a man-servant looks after his master. The masters are set apart from their servants by their way of life, their behaviour and their interests and they do not usually share the secrets of their work or their personal plans with them. The soul and spirit, too, act without necessarily revealing their motives to the heart and mind.

But if a maid always behaves herself perfectly, her mistress will begin to trust and confide in her, and talk to her about her plans, her happiness and her love for her husband, the spirit. When this happens the maid, that is, the heart, is overjoyed to know that her mistress trusts her enough to confide in her. Similarly, if the man-servant works so well that he earns his master's trust, he too will begin to benefit from revelations from his master and become more enlightened and more clear-sighted. But before this can occur, the maid and the man-servant have to live together in perfect peace and harmony in the service of their masters. If they quarrel, if one of them wants this and the other wants that, their lack of harmony will disturb the work of the soul and spirit.

There are a great many more combinations and applications of this image which you should meditate on, for every condition of health or sickness, happiness or suffering, can be explained by the relations that exist between these four occupants of your 'house'.

So now, this is quite clear : the couple formed by the heart and the mind is a replica on a lower level of that formed by the soul and the spirit. Mind and spirit are masculine principles whereas heart and soul are feminine principles. The union of these two couples, heart-mind and soul-spirit, produces children. The union of mind and heart gives birth to acts on the physical level while that of soul and spirit gives birth to acts on the divine level.

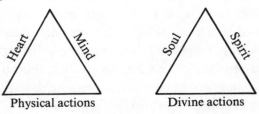

Figure 3 – The two 'couples' in man

The relationship between these four principles explains why the heart and the intellect are incapable of doing anything right if they are not subject to the soul (which represents divine love) and the spirit (which represents divine wisdom). When they have developed along the lines of love and wisdom, then they will become the son and daughter of God, but at the moment they are no more than servants. A son accomplishes the will of his father and the daughter the will of her mother. So, when the mind and heart are capable of accomplishing the divine will, that is of acting in accordance with love and wisdom, they will be the son and daughter of God. As long as they continue to be insubordinate and suspicious, driven by fear and a spirit of rebellion, they cannot be the son and daughter of God, only of man.

If the intellect is not purified by the light of the spirit it becomes a prey to pride. If the heart is not purified by the warmth of the soul it lets itself be led astray by passions. And it is precisely in this that human beings have gone most seriously astray: they have broken off communications between the lower level of the heart and mind and the sublime regions of the soul and spirit, so that now, deprived of this life-giving link, their hearts and minds are ravaged and tormented. Only one thing can save them and that is to restore the bond with their masters and become honest, faithful servants. Then, once again, the heart will become a conductor of the soul, freeing the way for divine love to pour through it and the intellect will be a vessel filled with divine wisdom through which the spirit can manifest itself.

'You shall love the Lord your God with all your heart, with all your soul, with all your mind, and with all your strength'. The implication of these words is that all of man's faculties should be placed at the service of Almighty God. The question is, 'How?' Peter Deunov answered this question when he said, 'Have a heart as pure as crystal, a mind as luminous as the sun, a soul as immense as the universe and a spirit as powerful as God and united with God'. This means that we must love God with the purity of our heart, the light of our mind, the immensity of our soul and all the power of our spirit.

The heart must be pure. This means that our hearts must be cleansed of all selfish feelings, desires and appetites that turn it into a swamp of stagnant, muddy waters incapable of reflecting Heaven. The mind must be bright and shining in order to light up our path. The soul must be immense, and it is love which makes the soul grow and expand. When you are full of love you feel capable of embracing the whole universe. The spirit becomes strong and powerful when it is in communication with its Creator, the one and only Source of true strength. The sad thing is that, instead of putting these faculties at the service of God, as they should, men and women often put them at the service of other human beings, and this is their downfall!

Suppose someone comes to you and says, 'Dearest, give me your heart. I need it!' You will probably begin by refusing, but if he starts to weep and beseech you, day after day, for weeks or months, in the long run you give him your heart. So then he will strut about with two hearts, but you will not even have one! Or suppose someone else comes along and insists that you give him your mind because he needs it for his work. He is so insistent that, after a few weeks or months, you give it to him and then you have no mind of your own. Yet another comes along and tells you he loves your soul, so you give it to him, and then you have no more soul. And, finally, someone comes and asks you to give him your spirit, and there, again, you end by giving it to him. And that is how you get the reputation of being very charitable!

Why are you so surprised? Do you think that it is not possible to give away one's heart, mind, soul and spirit? Oh, but it is perfectly possible! In fact it is very easy to do so, and you would be horror-stricken if I told you that there were not very many human beings who have not already given away or sold their hearts or minds in exchange for money, pleasure, power or fame. The inhabitants of the lower reaches of the invisible world are very anxious to get hold of the hearts and minds, souls and spirits of human beings so as to use them for their own works of darkness. Actually, these creatures cannot subjugate a man's soul and spirit for they are of divine essence; they can only capture their hearts and minds. Or if, as sometimes happens, they do manage to enslave a person's soul and spirit for a time, it is because they were too warmly associated with the heart and intellect, for these two are much closer to the material plane and, therefore, much more easily influenced by inferior forces. But this enslavement cannot last, for the soul and spirit are free and invulnerable except, of course, in the case of someone who deliberately makes a pact binding himself to the Devil for all eternity.

But the higher spirits of the invisible world also seek to manifest themselves through man. These are the spirits who form a hierarchy of angels and archangels all the way up to the Godhead, and it is to them, and to them alone, that we should give our minds, hearts, souls and spirits. With them we can be sure of being in good hands; they will never rob us, never cheat or abandon us. We must beg them to come and use us for the glory of God and His Kingdom.

Perhaps you will ask, 'What should we do if someone comes and asks for our heart or our mind?' The answer is very simple. Suppose you have a violin which you have tuned to your personal rhythm, your own inner vibrations, and someone comes along and wants you to give it to him. You should tell him, 'My friend, I'll give you the music that comes from my violin, but it's my violin and I intend to keep it. It wasn't made for you.' Or suppose again that you have some money in the bank and someone wants you to give it to them; you must tell him, 'My friend, I'll give you the interest on that capital, but I intend to keep the capital so that it can go on earning interest.' Or suppose you have a fruit tree in your garden and someone wants to dig it up and take it to his own garden; you must tell him, 'My dear fellow, I intend to keep that tree in my garden because that's where it belongs, but you can come and eat its fruit to your heart's content. In fact I'll give you a cutting to plant in your own garden. But that's all. You can't have my tree.' And, finally, suppose you have a rare and extremely valuable book and the same scenario takes place: someone wants you to give it to him. You will say, 'You can come and look at it every day if you want to;

you can read it and copy it as much as you like, but the book must stay in my library because I'm very attached to it.' If you do this you will be giving all these people some work to do which will get them out of their habits of laziness. They will all make progress and everyone will be satisfied!

It is now up to you to make the connection between these examples and what part of your heart, mind, soul and spirit you can give others. Don't give away your heart; give only your feelings. Don't give away your mind; give your thoughts. Don't give away your soul; give the love that emanates from it. Don't give away your spirit; give the beneficial forces which flow from it.

II

If I were to ask you, 'Can you do the four fundamental operations?' I feel sure you would exclaim, 'Of course, everyone knows how to add, subtract, multiply and divide.' Well, I am not too sure about that; these operations can be extremely difficult. Have you never had to suffer from having unwisely 'added up' with someone and then finding that you don't know how to 'subtract' yourself from the situation? The part of us which adds is our heart. The heart only knows how to add, and it is always adding things and getting them all mixed up. The part of us which subtracts is the intellect; the soul multiplies and the spirit divides.

If you observe how human beings behave in the different periods of their lives you will see that a baby touches everything without discrimination, he picks up, sucks and eats whatever he can lay his hands on, even dirty, harmful things.

Childhood is the age which corresponds to the heart and to the first operation: addition. As the child grows older his intellect begins to develop and he rejects whatever is useless, distasteful or harmful to him: he subtracts. Later again, he launches into multiplications: his life is full of women, children, branch offices and acquisitions of every sort and kind. And finally, when he is old and beginning to think about moving on to the next world, he makes a will and leaves all his possessions to others: he divides.

To begin with we accumulate; later we discard much of what we have accumulated, then we have to plant all the good that we have kept so that it shall multiply. If we don't know how to plant our thoughts and feelings, then we don't truly know how to multiply. If we know how to plant, then there will be multiplication and we shall have a rich harvest; after that we can divide, that is to say, distribute the fruits we have harvested.

Throughout our lives we are constantly in the position of having to effect one of the operations. Perhaps there is something troubling our hearts and we find ourselves unable to 'subtract' it; or our intellect rejects a good friend on the grounds that his learning and his social position are not good enough. Sometimes we multiply the bad things and neglect to plant the good things. So, you see, you have to begin to study the four operations in life itself. Once you have done that there are others to be studied: powers, square roots, logarithms and so on. But, for the time being, it is enough to study the four fundamental operations for, so far, we have not even learned how to add or subtract correctly. Sometimes we do an addition by nourishing a very base desire, at other times we subtract from our minds a good thought, a high ideal, simply because the first person to come along has told us that with ideas such as that we are well on the way to starving to death! So, you see, we still have a lot to learn!

The heart, the mind, the soul and the spirit all live in the same house, the physical body, and sometimes they quarrel and argue amongst themselves, but whether they like it or not they are obliged to stay together; they cannot be separated. And each one of them works, in his own way, on the 'house', that is to say, on the body as a whole and on each of its organs and functions, as well as on the face. When someone puts on weight it means that the heart is predominant in them, for the heart only knows how to add. When he loses weight it means that the intellect is predominant and in some cases this is a good thing, and in others it is not.

In the past, people preferred to be fat, and nowadays it is more fashionable to be thin but there is a danger in both tendencies. A good-hearted person has a tendency to get fat, he is good humoured, jovial, magnetic; his heart, overflowing with kindness, always has the last word. But sometimes this excessiveness leads to sloth; someone who gets too fat refuses to go anywhere on foot, to exert himself in any way or to try anything new: his heart won't let him.

When the intellect predominates a man tends to get thinner. The intellect is associated with electricity and the repulsive vibrations of electricity drive away the molecules of matter and lead to a loss of weight. The best remedy for overweight, therefore, is to think! Every day you can read advertisements in newspapers and magazines for all kinds of slimming cures which are both dangerous and very expensive. Well, now I am offering you a cure which is not only very effective it is also very cheap: think! Yes, think a little more and you will lose weight. And if someone is too thin and wants to put on weight he will have to give his heart more work to do; he must calm down and become more charitable and more receptive to others. Perfect balance can only be found when the heart and intellect work with equal intensity. It is not good for either the intellect or the heart to predominate, especially the intellect because, as it does nothing but subtract, it will end by subtracting everything and there will be nothing left; no more kindness, justice or honesty, no more providence, no more soul and even no more God!

The four principles of heart, mind, soul and spirit also influence the features of our faces. The heart takes care of the mouth: the shape of our mouth is the result of our feelings and of the way in which our heart functions, whether well or badly. The mouth reveals our qualities of heart; it is the visible expression of the heart which, itself, remains hidden. The mind, on the other hand, shapes the nose or, if you prefer, it is the invisible model on which the nose is patterned. The length of the nose, its position in relation to the rest of the face, whether it is pointed or rounded, its colour and so on — all these things reveal the mental characteristics of its owner. The soul takes care of the eyes: it is the eyes which reveal the strengths and weaknesses of the soul. The spirit takes care of the forehead or brow: it is the brow which reveals the nobility, power and lofty qualities of the spirit or, alternatively, the vices which prevent the spirit from manifesting itself.

Fashioned as they are by the soul and the heart, the eyes and mouth are feminine elements, whereas the nose and forehead are formed by the mind and the spirit and are, therefore, masculine elements. This gives us two mothers and two fathers, and we now have to find the children for, in conformity with the laws of nature, there must always be children. If there are no children it is a sure sign that the masculine and feminine principles are not united. If different elements are simply mixed up together it is possible to separate them, but if they are combined they can no longer be separated. If oxygen and hydrogen are simply mixed together they do not produce water. They have to combine. Children are like water, they are the fruit of the combination of two beings. And the same phenomenon takes place within us: heart and intellect, soul and spirit, produce children on the physical level. The child of the heart and the intellect (mouth and nose) is the chin; the child of the soul and the spirit (the eyes and the forehead) is the dome of the skull.

The chin, offspring of heart and mind, reveals the willpower and endurance of its owner and his ability to function on the physical level. Its shape and appearance; whether it is square or rounded, prominent or receding; indicate a number of things. The child of soul and spirit is the highest centre on the top of the skull and it expresses the capacity to accomplish the will of God and to persevere in a divine ideal.

The four essential phenomena studied by physics: heat, light, magnetism and electricity, are also related to the mouth, nose, eyes and forehead. The mouth is related to heat, the nose to electricity, the eyes to magnetism and the forehead to light. The mouth, related to heat, also has a special relationship with the eyes which are related to magnetism: this is the relationship of the heart and soul. The eyes are mouths which absorb light, and the soul, like the heart, feeds on feelings, but feelings of a divine nature. By means of our eyes we absorb a higher form of nourishment, light, just as, by means of our mouth, we absorb physical nourishment. In the same way, just as the nose discerns scents, the intellect, enlightened by wisdom, discerns good and evil, and the spirit, which is related to the forehead, perceives the realities of the world on High.

Of course, things do not always work as perfectly as they should. Sometimes the mouth expresses nothing good because the heart is cold. Why do some women use lipstick, do you suppose? To mislead others. Their hearts are like ice, but they want others to believe that they are warm. They know by instinct that men judge them by the rules of physiognomy, so they try to attract them by colouring their lips. The message is, 'My heart is on fire; if you come to me you will be warmed.' But often enough, if anyone does approach he will be chilled instead of being warmed, because the colour was only on the outside, not on the inside!

If the nose becomes too electric it shows that its owner nourishes ideas in his mind which make him jumpy and bad tempered. When an electrical circuit is overloaded 'sparks fly' as they say ! The nose indicates how much electricity is at work in its owner. If it is the predominant feature in his face it means that he is domineering and has a tendency to impose his own views on others.

The eyes are indicators of magnetism. It is always advisable to look gently and peacefully on things, without boring into them. Sometimes it is the eyes which become electric and the nose magnetic, and that is not good. There must be peace, gentleness and kindness in the way you look at people, but without exaggeration, for if you express too much tenderness everyone you look at will start to pursue you !

The forehead is linked to light. If it is hot instead of being cool and luminous, it means you are ill. But heat and light are close friends : if your thoughts are wise and reasonable, your mouth will utter warm words, capable of warming and reviving cold hearts.

There are several signs on our faces, therefore, in the shape, colour and emanations flowing from our mouth, nose, chin, etc., which reveal our qualities and defects. It is all there, very legibly written in our features.

Now, let's look at another aspect of this question. When a child is very small he expresses himself through movement, but as his will is not sufficiently developed for him to direct or control himself, his chin is still small and unformed. As he grows older he lives principally in his feelings, emotions and desires of all kinds (the mouth); by the time he is an adult he has learned to reflect and use his discernment (the nose); later, he begins to multiply all that is good and useful in his life, working with his soul (the eyes), and finally, when he is old, he lives in the spirit, reflecting and drawing lessons from the events of his life (the forehead).

We can also read a man's destiny in his mouth, nose, eyes and forehead. If a person's mouth, nose and eyes are charming but his forehead signifies nothing good it means that he will develop and manifest his good qualities during the first three periods of his life but later, when he is old, he will show himself to be selfish, harsh and cynical and will even deny the existence of God. One sometimes sees cases like this. If the forehead is not shaped according to the laws of the spirit it means that, in old age, the person will destroy everything he had built up earlier. If someone's chin, mouth and nose are badly shaped, but his eyes are better and he has a beautiful forehead, it shows that his childhood, youth and early adult life will be mediocre and even disorderly but that, as he approaches old age he will be influenced by more elevated, more spiritual elements, and change his ways. The treasures signified by the forehead show themselves much later, towards the end of one's life.

But it is possible to take this question further still: we know that man survives only if he eats (solid matter), drinks (liquid matter), breathes (gaseous matter) and absorbs light and heat (igneous matter).

In our everyday lives, solid matter represents our acts; liquid matter represents our feelings; gaseous matter represents our thoughts, and igneous matter the activities of the soul and spirit. Each of these four states of matter, which are related to the four elements, correspond to a particular phenomenon of nature: solid matter corresponds to earthquakes; liquid matter to storms and floods; gaseous matter to gales and hurricanes, and igneous matter to fires. All these phenomena are present in our lives, for we are constantly exposed to accidents and trials, whether physically or symbolically, from earth, water, air and fire.

We are exposed to earthquakes, storms, high winds and fires so that we can show whether we have understood the work we have to do with our physical body, our heart, mind, soul and spirit.

Peace, happiness and freedom will reign amongst men only when this work has been done. If everybody continues to talk about happiness and peace and does nothing to transform himself, the situation will never get any better. Peace can only come to the world through human beings who accept to work sincerely at their own betterment. Someone who establishes peace within himself, in whom all the different elements of his being dwell in peace together, only such a person is working for peace in the world. For the moment there is still a terrible lack of harmony amongst man's inner elements, and the wars we see on the outside are only the consequences of those raging within.

It is said that a wise man builds his house on a rock. A rock represents a solid foundation. What is this rock we have to build on? For the heart it is purity; for the mind it is wisdom; for the soul it is love, and for the spirit it is truth.

Ancient Persian tradition tells us that Zoroaster once asked the god Ahura-Mazda what the first man lived on, and the god replied, 'He ate fire and drank light'. There is very profound meaning concealed in this phrase and few esoterics have been able to interpret it because very few know the true nature and functions of the human soul and spirit.

The soul hungers and the spirit thirsts. The soul eats fire and the spirit drinks light. Fire is a masculine principle, the soul is a feminine principle and each one feeds on the opposite, complementary element. The soul aspires to a positive, active, dynamic principle: it eats fire. The spirit, which is masculine, needs the feminine principle, and it drinks light. Just as the masculine principle engenders the feminine (this is why Genesis says that Eve was formed from one of Adam's ribs), it is fire which engenders light.

In the beginning, God, the Primordial Fire, created light, the light with which it is said that He created the world. Light is always associated with matter because it is the raiment in which fire is clothed. In the sublime regions on high, light is associated with matter and fire with the spirit.

The soul, which is feminine, therefore, is nourished by fire, which is masculine and the spirit, which is masculine, is nourished by light, which is feminine. Similarly, the intellect, which is the son of the spirit on a lower level, prefers a feminine nourishment: thought; whereas the heart, which is feminine, prefers a masculine nourishment: feeling. Feeling, emotion, is a dynamic force, another kind of fire manifesting itself in the lower regions. It is a fire in reverse, in other words it is water. Observe the forms taken by water as it flows in streams, rapids and falls: they are exactly the same forms as those of flames, but in reverse. Water is simply fire flowing downwards. As for the mind, it feeds on thought which is feminine in essence. Thought is not so active and dynamic as emotion and this is why, incidentally, it is not really seen as a reality. What is a thought compared to an emotion? It has no force, it produces no physical effects, it doesn't upset things, whereas an emotion is a prodigious, awesome force which stirs matter into activity. In point of fact, thought and emotion are equally powerful, but on different levels. To all appearances water is gentle and obedient and you can do what you like with it. You can hold it in your hand and it will run off without hurting you. Whereas fire is quite a different matter! And yet water is just as powerful and strong as fire, but in other conditions.

The heart feeds on emotions and the mind on thoughts. But nothing is pure in these two regions of the heart and mind. There is always some sorting to be done, some dirt or dross that needs to be cleared away. Purity is to be found only on high, on the level of the soul and spirit.

The soul feeds on fire and the spirit on light. The soul inclines towards the spirit, it feeds on the fire of the spirit. And the spirit, which is fire, feeds on the light of the soul. Henceforth, keep this thought close within you, the thought of the Cosmic Spirit, which is fire, and of the Universal Soul, which is light. And when you meditate, concentrate only on these two principles, masculine and feminine, in their noblest and most sublime aspects of love (fire) and wisdom (light).

5

THE APPRENTICESHIP OF THE WILL

One sometimes meets people who, in spite of having very strong wills, have never managed to control either their gestures, or their thoughts or feelings. The reason, of course, is that willpower alone is not enough.

Let me give you an example. Suppose you want to control a machine: however much willpower you may exert you cannot do so, because you do not know how it is supposed to work nor what knob you have to turn to start or stop it. Control and mastery imply the need for knowledge: you have to know where the machine gets its energy from and then act on the right wire or the right switch. Once a machine has been started, if you don't know how to stop it, it will not stop; and if you try to stop it without knowing how, it will break you to pieces unless, of course, you break it first.

The same law applies in our inner life. You must never try to get rid of an energy which is bothering you by attacking it head-on. If you do that, you will be bound to fail and then, when you have tried two or three times, you will be convinced that the whole thing is impossible and stop trying. No, you must not give up, but you must realize that it is useless to get into direct conflict with your impulses and instincts. When you want to stir hot coals into a blaze, you don't put your naked hands into the fire, you use tongs. And when there is a leak in a water or a gas pipe, you turn it off at the main. Of course, willpower is necessary, but knowledge must precede it. As long as you try to solve all your problems by will alone without the light and guidance of knowledge, you will simply be wasting your energy.

In order to attain that mastery of all your gestures, thoughts and feelings, you have to begin when you are still young and practise in all the smallest details of everyday life. This is the only way to develop the psychic faculties you will need, later on, to master and control much greater forces. Perhaps you will say that you don't see the connection. Ah, well, that is just the trouble! As long as you have not learned to exercise your will to control the insignificant gestures of your daily life, you will never be capable of controlling your hatred, anger, contempt, disgust or thirst for revenge. If, at this moment, you paid attention to the way you eat, for instance, you would see that you are not even capable of controlling your hands. You sit there, fingering your knife and fork or crumbling a piece of bread, without even realizing that you are doing it. Begin by learning to keep your hands still. How can you ever hope to master forces which are so far beyond you if you cannot even control your own little movements? Do you want to collaborate in a really great work of some kind? If so, begin with the little things, because it is the little things which, one day, end by setting the great things in motion.

If you want to gain control of an energy which has already been set in motion, you have to go all the way to its source. Take an example: if you want to master a band of rebels you have to capture their leader, the head man, for it is he who inspires them and drives them on, and as long as he is alive and at liberty the others will carry on the fight. But once the leader has been taken prisoner his followers will not have the heart to continue. Therefore, before deciding to launch an all-out attack on a feeling, a passion, an attraction or whatever else may be tormenting you — which would simply make it all the stronger — you should sit down and think and try to discover the source of your enemy's strength. The simple fact of entering into yourself in this way causes forces concealed in your soul and spirit to come to the surface and help you to overcome your enemy. That one little effort on your part brings help from the divine world.

Apprenticeship in the art of mastery must begin very early in life, and it is up to a child's parents to see that it does. But as most parents have never practised control themselves, and have never tried to become models for their children, what results can they hope to get? Of course, people manage to control themselves to a certain extent when they are with others in a social context: it is in their own interest to do so in order to protect their reputation. So they take care not to say anything too outrageous, bite back the oaths that they would like to fling in someone's face, hide their feelings and become thoroughly hypocritical! But in their own inner sanctum they give a free rein to all their worst impulses and everything is ravaged and swept away by the flood! True self-control is not something artificial; it is not an external attitude which can be 'put on' in order to fool others, it is an inner attitude which goes very deep.

As long as you are unable to control and dominate yourselves, the cells of your bodies will refuse to obey you. They have to recognize the hand of a master on them before they will obey.

Even a horse can tell if the man on his back is afraid, and if he is, he'd better look out, because the horse will take great pleasure in throwing him! Whoops! A sudden shy and the rider is flat on his back and the horse trotting away, laughing to himself! Animals have no respect for someone who cannot control himself: they sense his weakness and bite or kick him. How often we have heard that Indian yogis can meditate for hours in the forest without being bothered by snakes or wild animals. Yes, simply because snakes and other animals sense the presence of someone who has attained self-mastery so they respect him. This sense of hierarchy is innate in all living creatures. If even wild beasts can sense your degree of evolution, how much more your own cells, which are like tiny intelligent animals.

Be assured that in this School you will never learn anything but the science of the insignificant! Yes, the science of what is infinitely small, infinitely despised, rejected and disdained. Why? Because that which is infinitely small opens the door to the infinitely great. Begin, therefore, by controlling your gestures and, first and foremost, your hands. You leave your hands to their own resources, beyond the fringes of your consciousness and this proves that your intelligence is not in control of your will. People can have strong wills and be very active, but their wills and their activity are not controlled. Sometimes one meets people with tremendous natural strength but who are incapable of self-control. They are strong, that is true, but with an untamed, uncontrolled strength which can be a great danger for society. Every form of strength must be controlled and directed so as to produce only beneficial results.

To complete what I have been saying I must add that if the will needs to be sustained by intelligence and knowledge, it also needs the support of love. The will is the offspring of the mind and the heart. Knowledge is not enough, therefore, to guarantee that your efforts will meet with success. Someone who wants to succeed in the spiritual domain has little chance of doing so if his efforts are not sustained by the love of something nobler, higher and more beautiful. It is that love which will enable him to overcome all obstacles.

When I see someone who imagines that he is capable of resisting the blandishments of his lower nature simply by his own willpower, I think to myself, 'Poor wretch; he doesn't know what's in store for him!' People say, 'Never again!' and before they know what has happened they have already 'done it' again! You must never say things like that, because when mischievous entities of the astral world hear you they immediately lay traps for you, and you are bound to fall headlong into them! This is why we often do exactly the opposite of what we have solemnly sworn to do. If I meet someone, therefore, who has no love for the sublime world and who boasts of being capable of overcoming temptation without it, I tell him, 'You have no friends or allies, so you'll certainly be defeated!'

So the first thing to do is to find some allies, to call on some heavenly entities to stay by your side and help you, then all the others will submit and begin to obey you, because you have the support of powerful beings on a much higher plane. But if you have no allies to back you up, how can you possibly expect to stand up against those forces which have inhabited you for hundreds and thousands of years? No one can stand up against them!

Well, there you are! This is something that no one has ever explained to you. So you struggle and struggle and then you fall ill! When you struggle you divide yourself, tear yourself in two, and it is very dangerous. An Initiate never struggles, he conscripts his negative forces and puts them to work. Thanks to his great love for something else, something better, more intelligent, more sensible, he manages to harness these negative forces. An Initiate never destroys himself by struggling as others do; he works, organizes and harnesses forces and this is the true science.

You must not count only on your own strength, your own willpower. The will is linked to love. If you don't love something you will never feel the desire to work to achieve it. You may work, but it will be forced labour and when one is forced, nothing ever turns out right. But if you love, then your will is there to urge you to seek and find the object of your love. So you have to link up with heavenly entities and win their friendship and support, for when the will is supported and sustained by love, by true, sublime love, then it is that love which prevents negative forces from making you their slave.

I have told you the same thing about beauty: beauty, like love, can be your salvation. Not just physical beauty, of course, but spiritual beauty which is also purity, harmony, intelligence and perfection itself: the beauty of God. If you have any feeling for that beauty you can never go and lose yourself in the sewers of the world. Someone who is wearing a beautiful, expensive suit is not going to start sweeping his garage or mowing the lawn or weeding the flower bed, because he knows he would get his new clothes dirty. But if he is already wearing a dirty pair of old jeans he will take pleasure in getting them even dirtier! Everyone knows this, so why does nobody draw the obvious conclusions for their inner life? Suppose that you have this sumptuous inner garment, by which I mean a pure, shining aura... Do you remember, I talked to you, one day, about Joseph's coat of many colours which is mentioned in the Book of Genesis? The story tells us that Joseph's father had given him this coat and that all his brothers were jealous of him as a result. In reality, of course, the coat is a symbol of his aura. In the Book of Revelation and in all Sacred Scriptures, descriptions of sumptuous, shining white raiment always refer to the aura, because it is the aura which is our true raiment. And now, suppose that your aura were extremely beautiful: if you knew this you would never knowingly run the risk of soiling it, so it is a protection for you. Whereas if you have already soiled yourself you will have no scruples about getting yourself dirty by playing in the mud!

Learn to cultivate your love of beauty and the divine world, therefore, every day: it is that love which will sustain your will and help you to overcome all obstacles.

6

BODY, SOUL AND SPIRIT

Christian theology divides man into three parts: body, soul and spirit, although in fact, very few people make any distinction between the soul and the spirit or know anything about the nature or function of these two principles or about the world in which they operate. If we compare this schema with that which divides man into seven parts (physical, etheric,[1] astral, mental, causal, buddhic and atmic), we see that the body corresponds to the physical and etheric planes, the soul to the astral and mental planes and the spirit to the causal, buddhic and atmic planes. The spirit, therefore, operates in three regions, the soul in two and the body, also, in two. The soul is in between the regions of the spirit and the body;

1) For further discussion of the etheric body, see *Christmas and Easter in the Initiatic Tradition,* (Collection Izvor No. 209), Chapter 6.

it is the link, the intermediary between the physical world and the world of the spirit. It is also the vehicle which carries elements from Heaven to earth and from earth to Heaven. Everything passes through the soul.

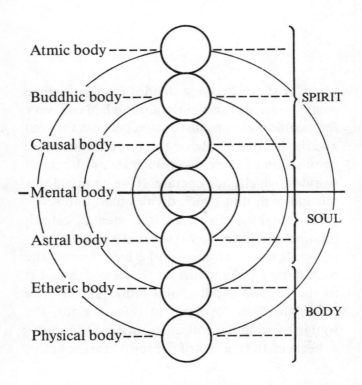

Figure 4 – The seven bodies of man in relation to the three divisions of Christian theology.

This division of a whole into three main parts can also be applied to a tree which has roots, a trunk and branches, and which is nourished by means of a network of ducts and vessels. The ducts carrying the raw sap from the roots to the leaves run up through the core of the trunk, and the vessels carrying the vital juices elaborated by the leaves run down towards the roots through the outer skin of the trunk. There are two currents, therefore, in a tree; an ascending and a descending current and the two never coincide. Similarly, in the circulatory system of the human body there are two circuits; arterial and venous, and these two must never meet or merge either, otherwise it causes the blue disease.

Similarly, the soul is that intermediary region through which currents flow between Heaven and earth. The soul is Jacob's Ladder, the ladder on which Jacob saw, in his dream, angels ascending and descending between earth and Heaven: this is the region of the astral and mental planes, the region of the soul. And in this region are two currents, that of feelings and that of thoughts, and these two currents never mingle or merge, either. No elaboration takes place in the soul, it is simply a passage-way, a channel used by entities and elements ascending Heavenwards or descending towards earth.

When the spirit acts on matter it uses the soul as its intermediary. The soul is an instrument of the spirit, a tool by means of which the spirit can make contact with the material world, for the spirit has to have an intermediary, it cannot act directly on the physical plane. Only the soul has the ability to touch the physical world, so the spirit works through the soul, to model and fashion matter, and transmit its orders. Without the soul and the possibilities it provides, the spirit would have no power over matter. The physical body is rich in all kinds of forces and elements: metals, crystals, oil, gold and precious stones — symbolically speaking — but the spirit can only use them with the help of the soul. The soul can slip in and out of the body because it is more — what can I say? It is not exactly more material, but it is closer to matter, so it can more easily be in touch with it and extract elements from it. And when it does so, then it can send them up to the spirit.

If so many philosophers and, even, theologians have spread so many complicated and totally false theories about the soul, it is because they have never properly observed nature. Everything is reflected in nature and when one knows how to observe it one finds answers to all the most complex and abstract problems. All the problems studied in Alchemy, Theurgy, the Cabbalah or

Astrology can be found, with their solutions, in physical phenomena. But you have to learn to read!

If we were to elaborate on all the possibilities of the soul we would, of course, find a great deal to talk about; it has tremendous plastic and formative capacities. We need our soul in order to fashion matter, whether to refine it and give it a subtler form or, on the contrary, to condense and concentrate it. These two operations are known to alchemists as *solve* and *coagula,* and only the soul can accomplish them. Neither the spirit nor the body is capable of this, only the soul.

And now, if we want to see how body, soul and spirit correspond to the different parts of our physical bodies, we find that the spirit corresponds to the head, the body to the stomach and abdomen and the soul to the two arms. This is an extremely interesting point, for the soul has two functions, that of condensing elements and that of making them more subtle, that of projecting them upwards and that of bringing them downwards.

These two processes are also represented by the Hebrew letter Aleph א . Aleph sums up in itself a vast science concerning the activity of the soul, the intermediary between Heaven and earth. And this becomes all the more meaningful when one remembers that Christ declared that he

was 'The Alpha and the Omega' which, in
Hebrew, is Aleph and Tav. 'I am Aleph'; this
means 'I am he who lifts the elements of earth up
to Heaven, and brings those of Heaven down to
earth.' Yes, it is Christ who causes the blessings of
Heaven to pour down on earth and the souls of
men to rise Heavenwards. If we want to reach
Heaven, to reach our Heavenly Father, we have to
go through Christ. Why have human beings never
learned to fit the pieces of the puzzle together, to
see the connection between different passages of
Holy Scripture and, thereby, reach a much clearer
understanding of exactly what they mean?

The spirit directs, orders and provides light,
but it cannot touch matter directly. That task
belongs to the soul which, under the orders and
guidance of the spirit, uses our hands to work on
matter, to mould and fashion it, to dissolve or
condense it, to heat or crystallize it. I realize, of
course, that when I say that the soul manifests
itself through our arms and hands, this may seem
to you a rather unexpected way of explaining
things. We usually think of the soul as manifesting itself through a person's eyes. Yes, of course
that is true too, because it can manifest itself in
any number of ways. But symbolically, the head
— and this includes the brain, the eyes and so on
— corresponds to the region of the spirit; of
course the soul is also at home there; in fact it is

at home in both the lower and the higher regions, but its own special region is not the head, but the hands. The spirit gives light, guides and ordains, but if there were no hands there would be no material realizations. Man does everything with his hands, with his soul.

When Jacob saw that shining ladder and all the angels ascending and descending on it, he was on the astral and mental planes. These two currents, the angels ascending and descending, the venous and arterial circulation of the universe, this is the soul. In man the heart and lungs lie between the head and the belly in the intermediate area which corresponds to the soul; and the arms are the manifestation of the soul as it reaches out to one side and the other. You see? The arms stem from the region of the soul. Everything has been created by Cosmic Intelligence with such marvellous correspondences. As for the eyes, ears, mouth and nose, they have all been placed at the top of the body, in the region of the spirit, because their task is to observe, hear, taste and understand things.

Of course, all that I have been saying may seem dreadfully theoretical. If you really want to know what the soul is you will have to go and see for yourself! One cannot really explain the soul, however much one tries, one has to see it for oneself. This is possible because the soul is material;

the matter of which the soul is made is so light, so tenuous and subtle, that it is usually considered to be invisible, but in fact it is not; it can be seen. The soul is a higher body, a body of light, but a body all the same. And the day will come when this body, too, will disintegrate and then man will live only as a spirit, for man's true essence, his true being is his spirit.

When we say that the soul is immortal we are really speaking of the higher soul, that is to say, the spirit. Man's lower soul will disappear, for it is material, and all matter is destined to disappear or, rather, to dissolve and be recombined differently. The soul, therefore, is composed of a very fluid matter which is constantly moving and breathing and which is so versatile and so full of life that it takes on every colour and every form. And these forms and colours can be seen. In fact, one can see that some people, in spite of all their jewelry, all their frills and furbelows, all their decorations and grease-paint, have murky, repulsive souls, whereas others, in spite of their rags and tatters, have shining, expressive, marvellously beautiful souls!

Yes, the soul is a reality, although many people nowadays who study psychology, the 'science of the soul', don't even believe in the soul! It is psychology without a soul, that is what is so strange! And, in fact, is it true, what they say:

that there is no such thing as the soul? Yes, it is true! Oh, I can see that you think that I am contradicting myself; not at all! You have to understand me: everything is true, but one has to see in what way it is true. If you find that something is true, then that is enough: it is true for you. If you say, 'God doesn't exist', then it is true; God does not exist in you since you do not believe that He exists. And if you say, 'There's no such thing as a soul', then that is true too; you have no soul, because if you had one you would feel it. If you deny that you have a soul then it means that you do not have one. Everything is always true; existence and non-existence, it all depends on what you can see from where you are standing. Jesus spoke about this when he said, 'According to your faith let it be to you.' This sums it all up!

All kinds of different definitions of the soul could be formulated, but the very best way of explaining it is this comparison with the trunk of a tree or Jacob's ladder. Once you have this image in mind you can say what you like: that it is a kind of electricity, a fluid, an emanation, a magnetism, a form of heat — all of these descriptions have some truth to them, but none of them points out the essential function of the soul which is to serve as an intermediary. I could even compare the soul to a pair of tongs! Yes, the kind of tongs you use to stir up hot coals in the fire. Perhaps you

would be shocked: 'How can you say such a
thing? It's an insult to the soul!' Not a bit of it!
The soul is the living pair of tongs with which you
can handle fire without getting burnt: an instrument, you see, an intermediary.

And now, once again, I want to show you
how I use the key of analogy. Since the whole of
creation is built according to one, identical structure or pattern, with only a few minor modifica-
tions, wherever we look we can find the same
three divisions: form, content and meaning, or
body, soul and spirit. Look at an egg... yes, an
egg: it explains everything. This, incidentally,
is why an egg is such an important symbol
in Initiatic tradition: it is an image of the
universe. What can you see in an egg? The
yolk which contains the living germ; the
white, that is the albumen, and the shell. The
yolk is the spirit, the white is the soul and
the shell is the body. The germ, therefore, is
in the centre, the white is in between and the
shell is on the outside. The structure of a cell
follows the same pattern. Every cell is composed
of a nucleus, the cytoplasm and an outer mem-
brane. And when you break the shell of an egg,
what happens? The white and the yolk run
out and the life is lost. So just as an eggshell
protects the germ of life in an egg, the human
body serves as a protection for the life inside

it, that is to say, the soul and spirit. When the body is broken, life departs, the soul and spirit escape.

But what is the soul? Just as the white of an egg contains the nutrients necessary to nourish the embryo chick, so does the soul contain all the nutrients necessary to sustain human life. But life itself belongs to the spirit. The germ is not in the white but in the yolk of the egg; similarly, life, true life, is found in the spirit, and it is this life that the soul sustains, nourishes and causes to circulate. How do I know all that? Simply by looking at what is there, before my eyes; nature has laid it all out for everyone to see!

You can see the same pattern in a grape: the seeds contain the germ of life of the vine in the same way as the nucleus contains the life of a cell; the flesh surrounding the seeds is the soul, and the skin represents the physical body. When you eat a fruit, therefore, you eat the life which is in the soul but which originates on a higher level, the level of the spirit. And what do you do with the stones or seeds? You don't eat them, do you? You plant them! Love, wisdom and truth are there: truth is in the seed, love in the part you eat, and wisdom in the skin, the outer wrapping. Yes, wisdom is what is written on the outside, that is to say, the form. Love is what we eat: life. And truth is what we plant to ensure the continuity of life. How clear it all is! In every fruit there is a spirit, a soul and a body.

But there is one thing which it is very important to understand, and that is that in spite of the fact that we always speak of spirit, soul and body as different realities, they are, in fact, of the same essence. The difference between them lies in their consistence, their degree of materialization: the body is a condensed form of the spirit, the spirit is a subtler more rarefied form of the body, and the soul lies halfway between the two. But if we question nature once again, and ask her where else we can find body, soul and spirit, she will tell us that they can be found in the four elements. The earth is the body; the soul is water and air, and the spirit is fire. And why is the soul made up of two elements? As I have already told you, the soul is twofold, it is the link between the two other components: body and spirit. In the same way, water is in contact with earth and air with fire. Water nourishes the earth and air nourishes fire. Water and air together, therefore, make up the soul which nourishes earth and fire. And the whole network of communications is here, too: both water and air ascend and descend.

As I have already said, the soul is composed of the astral body and the lower mental body and it is criss-crossed by two currents: the current of feelings or emotions and the current of thought. Water corresponds to feelings and air corresponds to thought. Water and air circulate in the zone that lies between earth and fire, and air nourishes fire: without air fire cannot burn; and water nourishes earth, for without water the earth remains sterile. So here you have yet another division, the division into four parts. There is no contradiction, however, between this division into four and the division into three. In nature, the soul is represented by air and water which, like the soul ascend and descend.

And now let us take the case of water: water is normally found in the liquid state, but it also exists in the solid state, as ice, and in the gaseous state in the form of vapour. It is still water, still the same substance, but in varying forms which differ in their degree of subtleness. In its normal state water is liquid, when it is exposed to low temperatures it hardens into ice, and when it is heated it is converted into vapour, but it is always the same substance. Ice is solid enough but this is only a form, a temporary appearance, since we know it can also become liquid or vapourous. In the same way, body, soul and spirit are one and the same substance in more condensed or more subtle states.

This is why alchemists used to teach that there was only one, fundamental matter, and that all the different forms of matter: metals, crystals, flowers, the flesh of animals and men, air, fire and so on, were all made of the one, original matter in varying degrees of condensation. How right they were! And this being so, what is the physical body? It is a condensed form of the spirit. And what is the spirit? It is matter in its subtlest, most diluted, most immaterial state. And this also explains why the alchemists used to say that all operations were possible by means of *solve* and *coagula*. How can this be achieved? By the use of heat. Heat acts on matter, giving it different forms and a different consistence, depending on the degree of heat applied. Fire, therefore, is the magical element which determines the particular form and characteristics of every material thing: gold contains a certain degree of heat, silver another and lead yet another, and so on. When an adept obtains possession of this fire, this magical agent, he can transmute lead, silver or iron into gold or, on the contrary, turn gold into iron or other metals. The only thing is, of course, that the alchemists' fire was not the fire known to glass-blowers and smiths, it was that secret, subtle fire known as the philosopher's fire.

And now, let us get back to the subject of the soul. The space between the egg-yolk and the shell, therefore, between the centre of a circle and its circumference, all this space is the soul. The spirit is an almost imperceptible dot, whereas the soul is immense; in order to nourish the spirit, the soul has to be inexhaustible. The spirit is hungry and feeds on the soul, so the soul has to have an endless supply of nourishment in order to satisfy the spirit. The spirit, however, in spite of all the nourishment provided by the soul, never gets any bigger, it is always just a dot.

Look at a lighted candle: it, too, can reveal many things. A lighted candle provides you with the four elements: earth, water, air and fire, and the three principles: body, soul and spirit. The body, or earth, is the solid wax of the candle; the soul is water and air, that is to say, the melted wax and the air which feed the flame. And the spirit, of course, is the fire, the flame.

If the flame is to continue to burn it has to be fed. But, as nothing can be nourished without the sacrifice of some other material, the candle diminishes as the flame devours it. It is the soul that feeds the flame and, in a candle, the soul is represented by water, the melted wax (if the wax refused to melt it would not nourish the flame) and by air, which is also indispensable to the continued life of the flame. The soul nourishes the spirit and the flame of the spirit rises in the shape of a Yod ‎‏יוד‏‎ , the tenth letter of the Hebrew alphabet, which is a symbol of the spirit!

So, you see, everything is clear and transparent. It all hangs together and no one element contradicts any other. And don't start objecting that there cannot possibly be any connection between a candle and an egg because they are not the same shape! The same principle is present in both, under different forms and with different combinations and applications. From only one thing the Creator has made multiple adaptations. And isn't this exactly what Hermes Trismegistus says in the Emerald Tablet? 'And as all things are One and come from One, by the mediation of One, so all things have been derived from this one thing by adaptation.'

Although, in the diagram of man's seven bodies which I mentioned earlier, the etheric body is shown as separate from the physical body, in point of fact it is not really separate. The etheric body is still part of the physical body, it is the subtlest, finest part, like a gauzy veil of dust or vapour: it is the atmosphere formed by the emanations of the physical body and it accompanies it at every moment. The etheric body, therefore, is part of the physical body, it is the vapour of the physical body, if you like, but it is not the soul. The soul comes after the etheric body, it is an even subtler region in which thoughts and feelings take their origin. And the spirit? The spirit is a replica of the soul but on a higher plane.

The spirit, too, is the region of thoughts and feelings, but thoughts and feelings of the greatest purity and light. Nothing inferior or impure can exist in the spirit, whereas in the soul there can be both good and bad. This is another point which is not at all clear in philosophy, and in the expressions of everyday life it is even worse: the word 'spirit' is used indiscriminately and quite inaccurately. The spirit of man cannot be evil or twisted. His intellect can be evil, yes. Even his soul can be evil for, as I have said, the soul contains both good and bad; it is the link between the body and the spirit and, as such, half of it is overcast by the body and the other half is illuminated and purified by the spirit. So any expression which implies that the spirit contains anything evil is based on a lack of understanding. The spirit can never contain the slightest trace of anything unclean or evil, otherwise it would not be the spirit. The nucleus is the guardian of life; it is always perfectly pure. The spirit, therefore, the spirit which comes from God, is absolutely pure and luminous. You must be sure not to get things mixed up.

And a flame, too, is a language. What does a flame do? It burns up all impurities, for there can be no impurity in fire; fire cannot tolerate anything which is less pure than itself. Water and air can be polluted, they tolerate impurities, it is only fire which cannot endure them: fire consumes all impurities. Earth, on the other hand, absorbs them; the earth is like a magnet, it has this special property of attracting everything impure and unclean and of cleansing and transforming it in its secret laboratories.

Soul, spirit and body — these three can be found everywhere in different combinations, but their correspondences, functions and applications are always absolutely identical. Do you want yet one more example of where you can find body, soul and spirit? Very well! Take the example of a bottle of perfume. The bottle is the body, the liquid is the soul and the scent which emanates from it is the spirit. The liquid feeds the scent; when there is no more liquid there is no more scent, only the empty bottle and, as no one values empty bottles, it gets thrown away. Similarly, when a man dies he is buried; when the soul and spirit have gone out of him and only the body remains, there is nothing left but to bury it! And why do people always take care to keep a bottle of scent tightly corked? Because if it stays open all the scent will evaporate. And the spirit, too, is very volatile; it feels 'bottled up' in the body and is always longing to escape. It is extremely jealous of its freedom and eager to return to its homeland, to the Fountainhead. This is why, in order to keep it down here, on earth, we have to give it the food it requires: the soul, and keep it tightly bottled up in the body. Is all this clear to you now?

When we eat, the coarsest part of our food serves to form and consolidate the physical frame, whereas the soul of the food enters the blood which circulates throughout the body in order to vivify it. We see the same principle at work everywhere: it is the blood, the liquid, that is to say the soul, which nourishes. And where can we find the spirit? The spirit is in the nervous system. And here again you have the three: body, soul and spirit, reflected in the digestive system, the circulatory and respiratory systems and the nervous system. And it is the blood which nourishes and feeds the whole body, even the nerves. This is why, when a man purifies his body and his blood, that is to say his soul, the activity of the spirit intensifies its activity and manifests itself in all its fullness. You see: everything hangs together.

7

OUTER KNOWLEDGE
AND
INNER KNOWLEDGE

For hundreds and thousands of years science and religion have been at each other's throats because they cannot agree on the nature of the world and human beings. In some periods religion has gained the upper hand and, at other times, science. In our own era it is science which is on top: for centuries it was reviled and persecuted almost to the point of extinction because, it was said, its discoveries were inspired by the Devil; so now it is taking its revenge, and it is the turn of religion to be vanquished. Perhaps you would understand the question better if I illustrated it with an image.

Imagine a huge, hollow sphere with one man inside it and another outside. Each of them describes what he perceives of the sphere: the man on the outside says it is convex and the one on the inside swears that it is concave. And now, suppose that this sphere is the universe. The man on the outside is the scientist who lectures and writes books to explain what he has observed. What he says is true, but only from one point of view, the external, objective point of view. The man on the inside is the mystic, the religious man, and he, of course, sees things quite differently but he too speaks the truth. How long is this conflict going to last? It is time now for a third person to intervene, someone who can present a global synthesis uniting both points of view. To the first man, the scientist, he would say, 'You there, on the outside, what you say is half the truth.' And to the man on the inside he would say, 'You, too, have half the truth; but it is I who possess the whole truth, because I know how to be inside and outside both at once. With my heart and soul I am on the inside, and with my mind I am on the outside.'

For the great majority of men of the 20th century, the objective, visible reality of what can be seen and touched and explored intellectually is more important than the subjective world of feelings, sensation or inner experience. And yet it is this subjective reality which is the most important because, in the final analysis, it is what you actually experience inwardly that counts, and not what is outside or alongside you. Reality is what you feel. If you feel persecuted, if you believe that you are being pursued by thieves or monsters, even if they have no objective existence it makes no difference : you panic and suffer just the same. For you they are real enough ! Or imagine, for instance, that you are very rich and possess all kinds of treasures : if you don't feel rich inside, if you don't enjoy your wealth or profit from it, it is as though it did not exist. When all is said and done, therefore, one is obliged to acknowledge that it is the inner, subjective world which is the most important; yes, what you feel and experience inwardly. If you are full of joy and feel that you are living in abundance, does it matter much if, objectively, you don't have a penny to your name ?

The most important, therefore, is the inner reality. This is simple and obvious, and yet the majority of human beings have still not understood it, with the result that they keep trying to live the outer reality. The trouble is that you can see, observe, draw pictures, etc. of the outer reality, but you cannot *live* it. Or, perhaps I should say that in order to live it you need to have certain inner dispositions in advance, for it is extremely difficult to do so. Someone, for instance, who has no inner sense of beauty will be completely indifferent to the glories of nature, whereas an artist vibrates instantly at the first glimpse of a beautiful view or a lovely face, and begins sketching or writing or composing music in his head, because a wealth of beauty is already alive within him.

But how does one convince human beings of such simple and obvious truths? They are only interested in possessing and accumulating more and more material wealth, and in this way their perception of subtle realities is blunted. They *have* a lot of things, yes; they *possess,* but joy and the zest for life abandon them. So many men are always trying to make new conquests, thinking that they will end by finding the one woman who can make them happy. They do nothing to cultivate their inner powers of perception; they imagine that if they keep looking around them they will eventually find satisfaction. But they won't! I have met so many men and women who are desperately trying to find love outside themselves because they are incapable of inner feelings! Yes, they are inwardly paralyzed. You must learn not to count so heavily on external things and use all the little opportunities that invite you to taste the things of Heaven.

When a boy and girl first begin to love each other they live in such a poetic state that the smallest token, a rose petal, for instance, from his beloved puts the young man into an ecstasy of delight and he keeps it always on him as his talisman. And yet, what is there in a rose petal?

Nothing, perhaps. But when he breathes its perfume it is as though he were breathing the fluids emanating from his sweetheart, her soul, her thoughts, and he imagines himself a poet, a knight in armour, a conquering hero for love of her ! Perhaps not a single kiss has passed between them, but the smallest thing, a look, a touch of the hand, is remembered and fills their dreams and thoughts for days and days; they feel as though they owned the whole universe. But once they begin to have a closer physical relationship, once they begin taking 'allopathic doses' of each other, they lose their subtlest sensations, something within them is blunted and fades. Then, in an attempt to recapture the delightful sensations they once had, they start to increase the 'dose' or to have other love affairs. But this is no solution : they simply lose their sensitivity; like those who lose their sense of taste by eating heavily several times a day. They become gluttons who have no true appreciation of the food they eat.

As human beings do not know these laws they do themselves a lot of harm. They must learn to return to the use of the homoeopathic dose for it is far more effective. How can you explain this ? It is because a homoeopathic dose can be perceived by the subtle bodies. As there is more space between the particles of the subtle bodies they are able to vibrate more readily. Homoeopathic doses, therefore, affect the subtle bodies, whereas allopathic doses only affect the physical body. In fact, to have any effect on the physical body, you have to administer massive doses, and when you do this the subtle bodies do not react at all. This is a law. A homoeopathic dose does not have much effect on the physical body because the particles of the physical body are too tightly compressed, too compact. In order to have any effect on them you have to use large doses. Whereas the etheric, astral and mental bodies, which are tenuous and subtle, are affected by homoeopathic doses.

You will ask, 'But then how do these tiny doses have an effect on the physical body'? The answer is that they do so through the subtler bodies. You have quantities of examples of this in everyday life. What is a look or a word? A homoeopathic dose! Suppose someone has thrown you a look of pure hate or said something wounding: you are so affected you are almost ill. And yet he never laid a finger on you! What has happened to affect your physical body to such an extent that you feel ready to die? It is simply that the message has been transmitted by your astral and mental bodies: that look or those words provoked such a feeling of desolation or horror in your subtle bodies that it was communicated to your physical body. On the other hand, if you are worn out and depressed and a friend comes to see you, you feel the warmth of love in his eyes and the kindness in his words, and you are on your feet again in no time! He has given your subtle bodies a homoeopathic dose which they, in turn, pass on to your physical body and then certain currents and communications are restored and you feel better.

But let us get back to what we were saying about the heart and the intellect. As I said, the intellect works on the level of objective facts and it possesses fifty per cent of the truth. And yet, considering its relatively greater importance, the heart, that is to say one's feelings, what one actually experiences, should have more than fifty per cent, because it is far more important to 'live' something than to learn it or read it in a book. Life is more important than learning. You can, of course, know many things with your intellect, but they remain superficial and theoretical, they don't touch the depths of your being. The things you learn intellectually are recorded in your brain, but on a superficial level, so they can very quickly be wiped out: one day they simply leave you and you forget them. Look at all the things you have already forgotten about the books you have read! And yet, at one time they were recorded on your brain! Yes, but only on the surface, and whatever remains on the surface can very easily be erased. And now compare that book-learning with something that you have actually experienced, something that you have felt and tasted deep down : whatever else happens to you in life this is something you can never forget. It is impossible ! Why ? Because it is recorded at a much deeper level, at the very heart of your being.

Nine tenths of humanity spend their time on the surface of life ; they don't live, they don't feel — by which I mean that they don't live or feel what is essential. They read about it, they discuss it, but they don't really and truly experience it. You have to live things and experience them on a deep level, then they will stay with you eternally. Yes, the only things you can take with you and which will never be wiped out even when you die, are those that you have verified for yourself in your own life, your own soul, your own heart. All the rest, everything you have learned at the university or from books, will have to be left behind when you leave this world. You cannot take all that knowledge with you because it is not really yours, it has never really become your own flesh. It belongs to others, you took it or they lent it to you, and one day it will leave you : you cannot take it with you. And when you come back to this world you will not be able to dispose of it at birth, you will have to go to school and read books and learn all over again: what a waste of energy!

This is why human beings are obliged to learn the same things over and over again, at each reincarnation. They cannot remember what they had learned in previous incarnations because they knew it only intellectually, superficially, on the outside of their beings. Whereas Initiates take care to pick out the essence of reality and assimilate it into their lives. They reject all the rest because they know that if they do not do so consciously and deliberately they will be obliged to do so when the time comes for them to leave the earth. If you assimilate what you know into your life, if you actually get the taste of it and verify it by putting it into practice until it becomes your lifeblood, your quintessence, then it will be truly yours and no one will ever be able to take it away from you. When you come back to earth you will bring it with you; you will not be obliged to begin all over again from the beginning, but will be able to go on adding true knowledge to that you already have.

Now, I am not telling you not to read or study. On the contrary, you have to do both. When you come here, to this Initiatic School, you begin by studying and learning many things, because you obviously cannot really feel or taste the truths that are taught here if you do not know anything about them. The difference here, though, is that you are constantly urged to emphasize life itself. And this is what makes everything different: no one advises you to collect and store up all sorts of different — and perfectly useless — bits of knowledge so as to become a walking encyclopedia! You are given some materials, of course, in other words you receive instruction, but it is up to you to choose what suits you, what is compatible with your particular temperament and, above all, it is up to you to put it into practice in your lives so as to build something essential within yourselves.

Generally speaking, human beings do not use their knowledge to build anything useful. It is strewn all over the place, in their filing cabinets and bookshelves, and there it stays. This is another weakness that I detect in all men of letters: they do nothing constructive with their knowledge. They are journalists, authors, lecturers, etc., so, of course, they do do something with it. They write novels or articles or they teach students; but they do not construct their own house, their own temple, that is to say, their own future.

I give you all kinds of information, therefore, but it is you who have to choose the materials and methods you can best use. I have to lay out all kinds of fruit and vegetables on the table — symbolically speaking — and it is up to you to take whatever suits your taste and your capacity ! Just because I display a great variety of 'dishes' it does not mean that you have to eat everything and make yourselves sick. No, choose just three or four exercises or methods, put them into practice all your life long and you will get fantastic results from them, far more so than if you tried to apply thousands of different methods. This is how I worked : I picked out only a few truths. But those I picked included all the others, they lie at the heart of all truth, and in this way, when I put them into practice I am in touch with the whole universe. I take care not to scatter myself far and wide because I know that when one is scattered one accomplishes nothing.

You understand, now, why I always emphasize how important it is to learn to feel things, to get the taste of things and then put them into practice, and not to be content with the surface, the objective aspect of things.

Make up your minds, therefore, that you are going to live the truths you receive while you are here, because if you don't put them into practice in your lives you will not be allowed to take them with you, and when you come back in your next incarnation you will be obliged to start again from scratch. Certain musicians, for example, play their instruments without really living their music on a deep, inner level, with the result that, in spite of having once been renowned musicians, when they reincarnate they are obliged to begin their apprenticeship all over again from the beginning. Whereas musicians who have really lived their music, take their talent with them and, when they come back to earth, they compose their own music when they are only five or six years old, like Mozart. And others are mathematicians from a very early age because, in a previous incarnation instead of being content to study mathematics intellectually, they really lived it. Perhaps you are surprised that I say you can live mathematics, but there is really no reason to be surprised. We can live the most abstract realities, realities that are far, far away from us : we can live them, touch and taste them and apply them in practice. But people don't live these higher realities, they discuss them and study a few facts but they don't *live* them, with the result that they don't *know* them. You could compare their attitude to that of someone who is always talking and writing books about love but who has never really loved anyone ; he knows nothing about it ! The day he falls in love he may no longer be capable of saying or writing anything coherent, but at least he will know what love is.

The secret of true intelligence is to understand, to feel and then to act in accordance with that broad, deep inner grasp of reality, with that deep feeling that cannot lie. True intelligence is intuition, for intuition does not have to be backed up by research and calculations, it is instantaneous, it perceives and penetrates things in a flash and communicates its findings to you immediately. Intuition is both sensation and comprehension: it feels things and at the same time it understands them. It is a higher form of intelligence, therefore, and it possesses that first indispensable element: life. When one possesses this form of intelligence, when one loves it, believes in it and admires it, one understands things instantly, while others are still scratching their heads in perplexity. Yes, once one begins to see the two faces of reality: the inner, subjective aspect and the outer, objective aspect, one is amazed to realize how simple everything really is.

8

FROM INTELLECT TO INTELLIGENCE

Most human beings allow themselves to be guided by their impulses. In itself this is not a bad thing, but when a human being obeys his instincts he is behaving like an animal. And if, throughout the course of his evolution, man has become a being endowed with reason and the capacity for reflection, it is not so that he should continue to behave like an animal. You will ask, 'But aren't there times when it is perfectly all right to follow certain impulses?' Yes, there are, in certain circumstances, and that is what we are going to look at now.

In the beginning, man was a pure spirit, created in the image of God and he dwelt in the bosom of the Eternal Lord. But when he descended into the material dimension, that life of peace, bliss and light was buried inside him and he forgot it. And yet that past experience is etched into that region of man which the Initiates call the superconscious: this is the region of the future and also of the distant past; but the past that is recorded here is much more distant than the past that we have in common with the animals: it is the past of our life in Paradise. Man has to let himself be guided by certain impulses, now, so that this sublime world may rise to the surface again and manifest itself. But before this can happen a great deal of inner organization and purification is necessary in order to open up the paths that lead to this region. Only when this preliminary work has been done will man be free to release the divine currents of pure light, pure music and pure inspiration within himself — and then he will be free, also, to abandon himself to these currents. That is what great geniuses do, painters, poets and musicians. They abandon themselves to the higher forces which impregnate them. But when someone is capable of that it means, of course, that he has had to work and practise for a long time to open the channels for the higher currents to pass through.

In your present stage of development it would be better if, instead of abandoning yourself to the guidance of your impulses, you used your intellectual powers to control and dominate them. For this is the true function of the intellect: to control and master certain animal impulses which were perhaps excellent in the past but which can be really harmful today. When you go looking for work in a factory or workshop of any kind, you will be expected to be capable of control: no one will trust you with machines or delicate instruments if you do not know how to handle and control them. And why should it not be the same for what goes on in your inner being? You have to get into the habit of reflecting about what you do, of analyzing your acts so as to sift out the good from the bad and keep only what is useful and beneficial for yourself and others. This is the task of the intellect, and once this is done you will be able to give all those subtle forces, which are so much greater and more powerful than you, the means they need to manifest themselves: you will become conductors of Heavenly currents, expressions of the Godhead.

At the moment it is evident that human beings do not see the intellect in this light. Ever since they realized that the powers of the mind could be used to explore and, consequently, act on matter, human beings have cultivated the intellect as though it were supreme and this is why there are so many people in the world who are very learned and very gifted intellectually. But now we have to ask why, in spite of all their knowledge and intellectual development, human beings are not really any better. On the contrary in fact: the number of delinquents, criminals and mentally handicapped is constantly on the increase. Hate, cruelty, aggressiveness and violence are cultivated everywhere. Civil disorders, rebellion and wars are more and more common all over the world. One cannot help wondering how it is that the intellect is not only powerless in the face of these manifestations but even seems to foster them.

One meets any number of highly educated people who are extremely well informed in every area, but whose lives are just as undisciplined, dishonest and corrupt as those of the ignorant. In fact they are worse, because their knowledge makes it all the easier for them to succeed in their shady undertakings. There is one absolutely essential point which has escaped them: they have developed their intellect and their capacity for information to such an enormous degree that they have not felt the need to cultivate, at the same time, a faculty that could animate all that knowledge. And now everybody is caught up in the system, even those who believe in the spiritual dimension; they have been so 'intellectualized' that they no longer have any truly spiritual life or radiance: nothing in them awakens an echo of the divine in others. They are as cold as ice because they are all intellect and it is normal for the intellect to be cold, it is not lively and animated.

Learning is a good thing, but it cannot save the world, on the contrary: the more learning men have the more they use it as an instrument to subjugate and dominate others. You only have to see how all those clever, efficient 'graduates' behave. 'Oh', you will object; 'it's because they're naturally boorish, not because they're knowledgeable.' No, no! It is because they know too much, or rather because their knowledge is all turned in the wrong direction: all it has done is to reinforce their lower nature. This is so true: everything they learn can be used to serve their lower nature; no one ever gives them the kind of knowledge that would enable them to take their lower nature in hand and learn to dominate it. Their knowledge supplies them with arms but not with an ideal of self-improvement and so, of course, they use those arms to satisfy their basest appetites.

It is quite extraordinary to see what effect learning has on most human beings: they immediately consider themselves superior beings and become proud, haughty, ambitious and cruel. Oh, yes! That is true and it is very bad. Even if you know everything that can ever be known on earth you must be simple, warm and friendly towards others.

How can anyone fail to see that it is the excessive development of the intellect that is bringing ruin on mankind? I know the history of the human race and I know that several human civilizations have already been wiped off the face of the earth because they had taken the very same direction that we have taken, today: the intellectual faculties developed to excess, too much knowledge and not enough spiritual qualities. This is why they did not survive. Learning which is not animated by the spirit can only lead to destruction.

I have met some extremely talented people in my life and been lost in admiration of what they could do, but I have noticed that the only thing that mattered to them was to cultivate their talent, and that, in my opinion, is where they betrayed their limitations. It is admirable to have a talent, but one must not think that it is the be-all and end-all, and look no further.

Human beings can be divided into six categories: brutes who are not far removed from the level of animals; ordinary men; men of talent; men of genius; saints, and, finally, Masters, Initiates who are close to the level of angels. The man of genius is well above the man of talent, but a saint is superior to a genius because he possesses purity and love, and this is not always the case with a man of genius. And what about a Master? Why do I put him above a saint? A saint is pure and he lives in the light of heavenly love, but he does not necessarily possess either knowledge or power whereas a Master is already a saint and has also developed knowledge and spiritual powers.

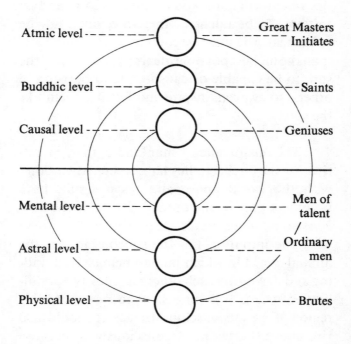

Figure 5 – The six categories of human beings

It is not enough to develop one's talents for, as you can see from the diagram in Figure 5, talents belong to the personality and, in fact, it would be true to say that for most people, intellectual and artistic talents are simply an occasion to cultivate their personality. You have to go much further than that and strive to develop the qualities which will make you a genius, a saint and an Initiate. To be talented, therefore, must not be your ideal. You must be content with nothing less than the highest possible ideal : to become like the sun, to be capable of causing life to burgeon in others, to awaken, inspire and fertilize them like the sun !

The misfortune of mankind is that, in cultivating the intellect, they have severed their bond with the world above and, as a result, have become a prey to the obscure forces of the subconscious which never stop bombarding them with vile impulses. For the subconscious is the animal world in which human beings lived, killing and devouring each other mercilessly, for millions of years. It is time, now, to rise above this region of the subconscious. In fact we should also rise above the realm of consciousness, because there, too, man is influenced by the world below, and the intellect uses up all its energies in the attempt to satisfy the needs inspired by this lower world. Left to itself the intellect is not capable of working for a noble, generous ideal, only for the interests of our lower nature.

When faced with the problems of existence the intellect is inadequate. It is capable of reflection, it can see what is going on, but it cannot find the true solution. The solutions of the intellect are always inspired by very inferior motives: to hoodwink and cheat others, or to elbow them aside and ruin them in order to assert oneself. For this reason the intellect is not yet intelligence; it is still too egotistical and limited. True intelligence begins when man has learned to create a bond between his intellect and the higher world of the superconscious, when he is capable of controlling his thoughts and feelings and of using them for the good of the whole world.

All those who have learned how to work in this way have been capable of sublime accomplishments; amongst them are certain philosophers, scientists and artists and above all, of course, the Initiates. All the others, all the warlords and conquerors who laid waste the earth, must be forgotten, rubbed out — history does not stand to lose much — and we must remember only those who responded to the inspirations they received from the world above in order to help humanity to advance.

Remember this one thing, therefore: it is absolutely normal for man to use his intellect to accumulate knowledge that will enable him to work with matter, but all his activities must be inspired by the desire to bring the currents of the superconscious down into the conscious and, even, into the subconscious so that it may be cleansed and purified and all its wild beasts tamed. Only then can the intellect truly become intelligence.

9

TRUE ILLUMINATION

The disciples in an Initiatic School learn to arrest their thought processes in order to visit other regions which lie far above and beyond them and taste sublime sensations of ecstasy and bliss. Hindu sages say that the intellect murders reality, and it is true : it is impossible to know reality with the intellect. Thanks to the intellect we can know masses of superficial details, but never the reality, the quintessence. Only the heart has the power to penetrate reality.

The surface and the heart of things; the objective world and the subjective world, these are the two aspects of reality, and the intellect is designed to explore the objective world while the heart is designed to know subjective reality. But when Initiates speak of the heart, they are not talking about the physical heart nor about emotions or feelings. When Initiates speak of the 'intelligence of the heart', they are speaking of the soul with its capacity to sense the inner reality of things and grasp their quintessence. Any other kind of sensation, obviously, is not a reliable criterion. And yet so many people see everything in terms of their own sensations. Their sensations have a measure of reality, that is certain, but they apply only to their own particular case. At best, therefore, they are only partially true, and often false or morbid. As for those who react only with their intellect, they have absolutely no experience of reality. So one cannot rely on either one or the other.

Initiatic Science tells us that there are two kinds of thoughts and two kinds of feelings, lower and higher. On the causal plane which is above the astral and mental planes, thoughts and feelings melt together so that it is possible, at the same time, to feel and to understand. This truth is inaccessible to most human beings who know nothing of their own structure beyond a few manifestations of their physical, astral and lower mental bodies. They have no notion that there are higher ways of thinking, feeling and acting. Only someone who has already had some experience in this area, who has known ecstasy, knows that state in which thought stands still and another faculty awakes, a faculty which is both sensation and understanding but without the intervention of thought.

For my own part, all this is quite clear because Heaven has given me the ability to experience these states: I have touched and felt and understood. The problems begin when one wants to describe and explain these experiences to others, because they are moments in life in which one has lived in another dimension. It is impossible to make others understand. But I want you to understand at least one thing, and that is that you must never delude yourselves into thinking that you can know truth by means of the intellect alone. You have to awaken a higher intellect, which is not the intellect we all know but the spirit. In the same way, in order to feel things in all their fullness it is not the heart that has to be awakened, but the soul.

Most human beings are torn between their heart and their intellect without really understanding that although both are necessary and useful, they are not enough, that one must develop another faculty: the faculty of intuition. Intuition is at the same time intelligence and sensibility, but on a higher level. Intuition can reveal the whole of truth; it is superior to clairvoyance, for clairvoyance only gives you the objective view of the astral or mental planes: you see and what you see terrifies or enchants you, and that is all. Whereas with intuition you do not see anything but you understand things as though you were seeing them a hundred times more clearly and, at the same time, you live them, you feel them. Intuition, therefore, is superior to clairvoyance and it is intuition which leads to true illumination.

Many spiritual people, particularly in the East, attempt to attain illumination by creating an inner void. I am willing to believe that some succeed, but when I was in Japan, I lived for a time in a Buddhist monastery up in the mountains not far from Tokyo, and there I had the opportunity to observe the daily lives of the monks and take part in their meditations and exercises. The means of investigation at my disposal are, perhaps, very limited, I agree, but as far as I could see from my observations and by taking part in all their activities, I fear that the void they were seeking was really and truly a void. I have no wish to criticize, but from what I have learned of the true Initiatic Science, a void must never be a goal in itself. If a disciple or an Initiate seeks to empty himself it must be in order to receive fulfilment, and that fulfilment should normally be reflected in his face and in his whole attitude.

While I was in this monastery, therefore, I participated in their meditations every morning, very early, and again in the evening, and I was always very surprised to see how, after these lengthy meditations, there was no visible change on the monks' faces, no light, nothing! Perhaps they were tired? Perhaps they had reached a point of saturation after years and years of practice? I don't know. But in my opinion, after a lengthy meditation which has put one in touch with the divine world, one's face should express something new and luminous, something vibrant and expressive, and if it does not it means that one's meditation was useless. I repeat, emptiness is not a goal in itself. Its only purpose is to attract fullness.

Emptiness is the manifestation of the feminine principle and fullness that of the masculine principle. If the two are not joined, however, the whole thing is a failure. Take a flint (the feminine principle) and strike it with a piece of iron (the masculine principle). If you cannot get a spark and set fire to the tinder the operation is a failure, and a great many meditations are failures in just this way! You see? All the mysteries of the universe are revealed in the two principles, masculine and feminine. Whenever I want to understand something I call on them: 'Oh, Eternal Principles, Eternal Feminine and Masculine, come and enlighten me!' and they come and explain everything to me.

I insist: emptiness must be used to attract fullness, plenitude, otherwise it is useless and worse than useless: it is dangerous. Some people imagine that if they can achieve this void, this passive state of emptiness, they will be visited by the Deity. No, when someone is passive there is no guarantee that it is the Deity who will come and visit him. It is more likely to be negative entities from the invisible world who will be delighted to visit and settle down in someone weak and defenceless. Yes, for anyone who abandons himself without having first taken the trouble to protect himself by developing his active, dynamic principle, is at the mercy of the worst kind of entities.

When you meditate you should begin in stillness and peace, by relaxing and establishing a state of calm. After a few moments you can become active and dynamic, concentrating your thoughts and feelings on whatever subject you have chosen, and projecting and intensifying them until you feel yourself expanding and filled with a sensation of wonder. At this point you can pause and empty yourself, stop thinking and allow yourself only to feel, and you will be in no danger since you began by being active and outgoing; the malevolent entities who may have tried to slip in and drain away all your energies for their own benefit will have been repulsed. The only way to create a void without danger, therefore, is to begin by purifying oneself. What can you possibly hope to attract if you have not worked to make yourself pure and luminous? All your inner impurities will simply tempt undesirable entities from outside! Too many people keep praying for the presence of Heaven within them with no realization that this demands renunciation and sacrifice on their part — and they have never renounced or sacrificed anything in their lives! If only it were as easy as that! They clamour for Heaven at once, they want to be given all graces, virtues and gifts without any effort other than that of creating a void. Well, a void is the most dangerous thing there is if one does not know how to prepare oneself and ensure that one's emptiness attracts fullness.

The first thing you have to develop is activity and outgoing energy; only then can you safely explore the realms of passivity, mediumship and clairvoyance, because then you will be protected. But it is sheer folly simply to abandon yourself to emptiness in the hope that the Holy Spirit will come and fill your void. Someone will come, you may be sure, but it is not at all sure that it will be the Holy Spirit! If you have not worked very energetically to purify your inner self first of all, how can you possibly imagine that the Holy Spirit would accept to come and live in you? The Holy Spirit does not go and live in swamps! Other, inferior beings will accept your invitation because they will be attracted by the food you have prepared for them in the form of passions and lusts. But the Holy Spirit? Never! The Holy Spirit may come one day, but only after a very long period of profound, sincere purification, and when He does come you will receive true illumination.

10

THE CAUSAL BODY

If you want to get results on a spiritual level you have to climb up to the top of the mountain. The mountain I am referring to is your own mountain, your own causal body. You have to scale the heights of your causal body in order to rise above the mist and dust. 'Mist', 'dust' and 'mountain' are, of course, all symbols. Dust is that which clouds the mind when it has lingered on too many different paths, and mist is produced by the humidity of the heart when it is exaggeratedly emotional and sentimental and it, too, prevents one from seeing clearly.

In order to escape from the dust of the mind and the mists of the heart, we have to rise above the astral and mental planes and reach the causal plane. This is why, in your meditations and prayers, you should always try to rise, to rise very high, as high as possible. In fact, why not use your imagination and picture yourself scaling a mountain? The picture in your mind will lead you to another mountain, the one inside you, and when you reach the top, the causal plane, you will find so many more ways open to you for the realization of your spiritual thoughts and desires. In the Cabbalah God is called the Most High because, symbolically, power and omniscience are to be found on the higher planes.

Only he who builds his house on high ground is out of danger and that is why Jesus said that a wise man builds his house on a rock. The rock is a symbol of the causal plane. You are out of harm's way and nothing evil can reach you if you are very high up, on the causal level. Whereas if you build your house on the astral level, in the turmoil of your passions, temptations and volcanic eruptions — or on the physical or mental plane — you will always be vulnerable.

Jesus presented the same idea in a different form when he said, 'Do not lay up for yourselves treasures on earth, where moth and rust destroy and where thieves break in and steal; but lay up for yourselves treasures in heaven, where neither moth nor rust destroys and where thieves do not break in and steal.' I have already explained to you that the rust, moths and thieves are symbols: rust is the symbol of all the dangers that threaten us on the physical level, moths symbolize those things that threaten us on the astral level and thieves symbolize all that threatens us on the mental level. A disciple, therefore, has to rise above the physical, astral and mental levels where he will always be exposed and vulnerable and climb up to the causal level. Only the treasures which you have amassed on the causal level will remain intact for eternity.

So many people complain of being alone and left to fend for themselves, of being unable to count on anyone or anything! They had dreamed of having someone always at their side, ready to listen to them and help them when they were needed. But human beings, like situations, change. So it is much more sensible to meet others, associate with them and love them, yes! But don't count on their stability, otherwise you will be deceiving yourself and, sooner or later, you will be very unhappy when you find that things don't turn out exactly as you thought and hoped they would. This is true, even, for your children: you must know in advance that they will not always be as they are today, and that one day, in fact, they will leave you. If, by some happy chance, human beings behave as you hoped they would, so much the better: but don't count on it!

If you want to avoid useless sorrow and wor-ries, you have to realize that everything is con-stantly changing, everything is in the process of being transformed and that you cannot count on stability in any area at all. Once you have understood this you will never be unhappy again because you will never again deposit all your capital in a bank which is unreliable and doomed to failure from the outset, and you will concentrate on your own development, on becoming stronger and more enlightened: that is the only thing you can count on.

The way of wisdom is to count only on oneself; to rely neither on family nor friends nor possessions, but on that tiny divine spark which lives in each one of us and which we must nourish and tend so as to achieve, one day, true stability and true happiness.

This is the wisdom that Jesus summed up in those words, 'Build your house on rock'. Of course, this is symbolic, for even a house that is built on rock can be destroyed. What he was saying was: Don't look for shelter on the astral level. Don't put your faith in emotions, sensations and feelings, for on that level you will always be at the mercy of storms and hurricanes: there is no stability there. One day you will be full of good cheer and laughter and the next you will be in tears. Today you will be happy because you have found someone to love and tomorrow he will leave you and you will be heartbroken. And the mental plane cannot offer you any real security either, for how can you trust the flimsy concoctions or the shady schemes of the human mind?

The role of the heart is to counterbalance the intellect. There are people who have completely stifled all feeling; they function only on the level of the intellect. But this is not good either because they become completely dried up. Heart and intellect are both indispensable, but we must first find the right balance between the two and then try to live on a higher level than that of the intellect. One thing is important: when I tell you that you must not always live on the level of the heart I am not saying that you should live on the level of the intellect. Not at all, for the intellect is incapable of solving all your problems. Neither the heart nor the intellect are capable of that.

You cannot do without either your heart or your intellect: that is certain, but you can, at least, take care not to take shelter or set up house permanently in those regions. Your home must be much higher up, on the causal level. All you have to do is move yourself and your belongings up to a higher floor.

Of course, I know it is not easy to move house: generations and generations of people have built their houses in the lower astral and mental regions and they are accustomed to living in the midst of passions and tumult. It is terrible, sometimes, to see the places human beings have chosen to settle down in! And then they imagine that, in spite of all their ignorance they will be able to solve their problems! No, in those regions human beings have no possible chance of solving their problems, for they are too exposed to the wind and rain. Very few human beings have settled down in the regions of intelligence, love and peace so as to be sure of always being able to act freely. Of course, even they still have to face up to the turmoil and tribulations of life, but at least their true home is not there: their true home is up above.

As long as you do nothing to rise to a higher level, there will always be reasons for revolt, tears and complaints, especially if you remain on the astral level. Weeping and lamenting is no solution, and yet so many people are completely absorbed in their feelings! They take them out and show them to everybody, hoping for sympathy, compassion or approval from all sides. Really, human nature is very peculiar! Instead of being constantly preoccupied by your feelings, you must move house and go and live in that blessed region of pure reason, pure wisdom and pure light. All the methods you need are there; all the solutions you are looking for are there, but you have to go and find them.

And now, if you are wondering why we all have to put up with so many upheavals in our lives, I can tell you that it is because we have to learn what to think, what we can rely on and what we have to work at. All these tribulations, therefore, lead us to a much broader, more comprehensive and truer understanding. If you cannot see this you will have to stay where you are and suffer. But if you recognize that everything that happens to you is an occasion for you to rise to a much higher level, to ennoble and reinforce yourself and, above all, to become freer, then, instead of weeping and wailing you will be happy and grateful. You will thank the Lord, saying, 'Lord God, if it had been left to me to decide to climb all the way up to Heaven, I don't think it would have happened in this incarnation or even in the next. How good You are! I was floundering about in the morass and You have pulled me out of it. Thank You. Thank You. Thank You!' And you will welcome every new event as it comes along and try to see it in the light of your new understanding.

Instead of always exaggerating the reasons you have to complain or rebel, you must get into the habit of reflecting, reasoning, studying and moving up onto that higher level of the causal plane, onto the rock of which Jesus spoke. 'Well, O.K.', you say; 'If we're going to have to move

house we'd better get a car so that we can put all
our luggage into it.' No, you would do much better
to leave all that luggage behind: it is much too
heavy! It would be far better to take the time to
make new furniture and fittings, with other subtler, more luminous, more etheric materials. So,
leave all your precious period furniture behind
you and go and settle on the mountain peak
where matter is more reliable and longer-lasting
because it is purer.

You will probably ask, 'Where shall we find
that region?' and the answer is that you will find
it in the Sephirotic Tree where the causal plane is
represented by the Sephirah Binah. This is the
region of the Twenty-Four Elders of which St.
John speaks in the Apocalypse: 'Around the
throne were twenty-four thrones, and on the
thrones I saw twenty-four elders sitting, clothed
in white robes; and they had crowns of gold on
their heads.' The Twenty-Four Elders are seated
on these firm, immovable rocks, the Thrones,
from where they rule over the destinies of human
beings.

Binah is the region of Divine Intelligence or
Understanding. If you stay in the region of Yesod
you can be the victim of its illusions and mists.
Even the regions of Hod, the intellect, and Net-
zach, love, must not be your permanent abode.
You must go on to much greater heights, to

Binah. Once there, you can plant your tent or, if you prefer, settle down in your little caravan. For Binah is truly the Secret Place of the Most High mentioned in Psalm 91.

Now, of course, you have to understand all this correctly. When I tell you the meaning underlying these words of Jesus and of the Psalmist, I am not telling you to free yourselves from all your obligations to others. Your ties with other people already exist, you have signed contracts with them and you are not free to break those ties until you have fulfilled your commitments. It is no solution to leave one's husband or wife on the pretext that one wants to be free. If you do that you will simply incur other debts which will have to be paid in another incarnation. One cannot be free until one has paid all one's debts. Everybody wants to be free, I know, but you have to have the right notion of freedom, otherwise the more you try to free yourself the deeper you will sink into debt. It is not as easy as you think to free yourself. In fact, it is often when you want to be free that you begin to realize how thoroughly entangled and hamstrung you really are. Perhaps you imagined that if you severed some of your ties on the physical level you would be free? Well, you will soon find out that that is not the way: it often takes a whole lifetime to free oneself from certain memories or impressions, from certain images.

In fact a lifetime may not be enough. You may have freed yourself from a given situation, physically, but you still have a crushing burden within you which is holding you down.

No, you cannot solve all your problems in one fell swoop. Even if you do decide to move house, how long do you suppose it is going to take you? It is when you decide that you really want to do so, that you realize how firmly attached you still are. Picture a fish who decided it would leave its home in the sea or the river and go and live on dry land: the poor creature is bound to die. If it had wanted to survive such a change of habitat it should have got ready by acquiring lungs — and it has not got any lungs! If you want to move house you have to prepare yourselves. For even if you do manage to climb up to higher altitudes you will still not be able to stay up there if you have not developed the necessary faculties. You will have hardly reached the summit before you start fretting to get back to earth again, saying, 'Oh, I'm so bored up here! No cigarettes, no pubs, no night-clubs, and I'm just longing for a cigarette and a drink and a nice cuddle with a pretty woman! I want to go down again.'

Someone who wants to live in the sublime regions cannot indulge in such base needs. This is why not everybody is able to move house. Even if you got hold of some people and forced them to move to a higher altitude, they would give you the slip again just as fast as they could, because they would find it unbearable.

But you who are listening to me, try to find a way of setting up house on the causal plane. Human beings have been on this earth for millions of years and during this time they have evolved considerably, so that if you take the trouble to practise every day, to meditate, to get certain special cells in your brain to start working, you will come closer to the divine world. Then, once you get used to it, you will be able to keep moving just a little closer and begin to get a much broader, deeper and clearer vision of things until, one day, you will be capable of settling down permanently in these blessed regions.

11

CONSCIOUSNESS

I

That which we are accustomed to calling 'consciousness' could be defined as the meeting place, the focal point at which all the representatives of our psychic and physical organisms have agreed to convene. It is a little like the United Nations at Geneva. Geneva is the place where the representatives of all the world Powers, both friends and enemies, gather to meet each other and discuss and negotiate and try to solve certain problems and, for a time at least, Geneva becomes the consciousness of the world where explanations, negotiations and decisions take place. Similarly, consciousness is a neutral zone, a no-man's land, where, circumstances permitting, elements and currents of every sort and kind can gather to express themselves and have their say. You can also compare consciousness to a notice board or screen on which everything that takes place within a human being is posted or projected.

According to the degree of evolution of the person concerned, the nature and number of notices that are pinned up or projected onto this screen vary considerably. In a village in the past, the local beadle would go to the village square, blow his trumpet or beat his drum and announce two or three events of local interest: sales, purchases, decisions of the mayor and council, etc. The other villages of the region, of course, saw and heard none of these announcements. But if all those announcements were made in huge letters of fire in the sky, everyone in the whole world would be able to read them. Our consciousness can be restricted to the few announcements made by the village crier but it can also be as vast as the universe.

It can also happen that someone else manages to project his will and desires onto the screen of your consciousness, thus impelling you to accomplish them even without your being aware of it. You think that it is you who have made a decision and then acted on it, while, in reality, someone else has been using you, sending you orders from a distance, and all you do is carry them out.

It is essential, therefore, that human beings should be instructed in Initiatic Science so as to become masters of their own consciousness and not allow themselves to be swayed by all the forces and currents that flood into them from every corner of the world, nor even by those rising from their own subconscious. An Initiate, for example, cannot prevent certain obscure images or suggestions from reaching his mind in an attempt to hinder him in his work, but he knows how to dispel them. Whereas the consciousness of the common man is a screen on which all the most chaotic impulses manifest themselves, so much so, in fact that he never really lives his own life: he is always being badgered and trampled on, always torn by disputes and wars. For his belly, his sex, his heart, stomach, liver, and brain all send their representatives to the discussion tables, each clamouring for something different, and the result is an indescribable cacophony!

An Initiate understands that the individual interests of his different bodies and organs must converge in the interest of his whole being, so he imposes order and harmony amongst their representatives and, in this way, his consciousness becomes superconsciousness. In the common man, that which we call consciousness is often no more than a manifestation of the subconscious. All his hereditary and instinctive animal tendencies struggle to rise to the surface and project their own image onto the screen of his consciousness. This is why, when a disciple first sets foot on the path of Initiation, he must expect some surprises! He wants to pray, to be kind, to be pure, but he finds himself assailed by other desires, which object vociferously: 'No, no! Not that. We want something else!' The result, quite often, is that the poor fellow gives in. But if he doesn't give in, if he continues to resist these base desires, he will become progressively freer and more independent and begin to live on the level of the superconscious, because a multitude of heavenly entities are helping him and he feels sustained and enlightened by their blessings; in these conditions his consciousness will expand and receive more light. This does not mean that, from one minute to the next, he will be capable of breaking all his ties with the subterranean world. No! But through his own efforts and the fact that he calls on the divine world for help, it is as though he built a barrier between himself and the lower regions, and they no longer have the power to destroy the unutterably beautiful images projected onto his screen from Heaven.

But you will understand the question better if you refer to Figure 2 (page 33). As we have seen, the physical, astral and mental bodies correspond to our lower nature, whereas the causal, buddhic and atmic bodies correspond to our higher nature. We possess two natures, both of which have the capacity to act, feel and think, one on the lower level and one on the higher, and there is no real separation between the two. As shown in the diagram, each of the three lower bodies is linked to the corresponding higher body: the physical body to the atmic; the astral body to the buddhic, and the mental body to the causal body. And the goal of evolution is to reach the point at which each of the higher bodies incarnates in the corresponding lower body. Only then will human beings receive full illumination, because divine nature will then dwell within them. As for the boundary line between our higher and lower natures, this represents consciousness, the screen on which both regions, the individuality and the personality, are reflected.

Now, the whole problem is that, even when a man knows very well what evolution, liberation and self-mastery mean and what he should do to attain them, he almost always obeys the dictates of his personality. The reason for this is that his present level of consciousness is a product of his personality. He is not yet living in the supercon-scious, which is the level of consciousness of the individuality. If he had already attained that higher degree of consciousness characteristic of the individuality, he would have understood that every being is linked to all other beings, that they are one reality in that ocean of universal life which encompasses all creatures, and he would experience quite different sensations to those he experiences at present; sensations of joy, wonder and limitlessness. But as his present consciousness is a product of his personality and is rooted in the three lower bodies, it is necessarily restricted. Our self-consciousness depends on our thoughts, emotions and activities, but its scope is very limited, it is a consciousness of separateness; the self always feels itself to be apart and shut off from the Whole, apart from other human beings and from nature.

It is for this reason that all the exercises and spiritual practices taught in an Initiatic School are designed to enable you to establish a rapport between your higher and lower natures. One of the most effective of these practices consists in identifying with a heavenly entity: Christ, the Heavenly Father or the Supreme Mother. You will probably exclaim, 'But that is the best way to go mad!' Unfortunately, yes, there have been cases in which this identification wrongly understood has turned to insanity. It is a very fine line which separates an Initiate from a madman, just as there is only a fine line between a genius and a madman. Some people have taken themselves for Christ and gone out of their minds simply because they wanted to achieve Initiation without applying the right methods. If they had known how to use the methods correctly, they would have identified, really and truly, with Christ. Other, highly evolved human beings, have done so without losing their mental balance in any way. The great thing, therefore, is to learn certain rules and methods, and that is what you are doing here.

When you want to progress from the ordinary level of consciousness to the level of super-consciousness, represented by your higher Self, it involves such tremendous changes in your inner life that, if you do not know what methods to use in order to make the transition harmoniously, you run a great risk of provoking very serious disturbances. This has happened to many mystics and spiritual men and women who did not know how to set about it in the right way: they dived in head first, knowing nothing about the laws involved, with the result that their nervous system was thrown off balance or, without realizing it, they attracted the attention of malevolent entities and succumbed to their domination. This is why people have a tendency, nowadays, to consider that all spiritual people are a bit crazy!

You have to realize that the way we live and work tunes us to the wavelength of certain invisible entities, thereby attracting them to us. An Egyptian Initiate who wished to identify with the god Osiris or Horus, practised concentration, recited certain formulas and donned special vestments or masks and became, for a brief moment, the authentic incarnation of that divinity: it was because he had succeeded in vibrating on exactly the same wavelength, thereby enabling that sublime entity to speak and manifest itself through him. If you want to create a bond with another being you have to adjust your vibrations to his. This is a law of physics, and radio communications are based on this law.

Initiates, who knew this law long before the physicists — and understood it far better — knew that it was valid not only on the physical, but also on the psychic and spiritual planes and taught their disciples how to vibrate in unison with certain entities so as to receive messages from them. The entities could even speak through a disciple's voice and, often enough, when he re-entered his body he would be unable to remember what they had said. The same kind of thing occurs in certain cases of mental illness: without realizing it the sick person has made contact with entities of darkness or other negative forces which use them for their own purposes. Later, when the fit of madness is over, they remember nothing about the insane or criminal acts they have committed.

But let's get back to the question of consciousness. Generally speaking one could say that a man's consciousness is a reflection of what interests and concerns him, of his way of life. It exists only as a consequence of the many physical and psychic processes that take place in a human being. It is the screen onto which the pictures of his inner and outer life are projected. If your consciousness is tormented and a prey to anxiety and obsessions, it is useless to try to escape those anxieties and obsessions without changing your way of life. Otherwise it would be as though you watched a film and when you did not like the pictures, instead of changing the film you changed the screen! Consciousness manifests itself on the level of the brain, but it is a consequence of the activity of all one's cells. If we don't like what we see on the screen and want to change it, therefore, we have to change our cells and not the screen which only reflects their activity.

So many people complain of being tormented by certain mental images, nightmares and obsessions, and they have no idea how to get rid of them. They never seem to suspect that it is they themselves who have spent their last few incarnations making that film, and that now it is in the hands of an operator who is simply projecting it onto the screen of their consciousness. All those pictures which torment people come from a long way back. It is not our consciousness which has invented them; all our consciousness does is to serve as a screen, it is not responsible for anything it reflects, whether good or bad. The film was made long ago and now it is being projected, and one sees some scenes which are bright and very beautiful and others which are dark and shadowy. And as one cannot change that film, the best thing one can do is to start making a new one. At the limit, if a man is intelligent, what he sees reflected on his consciousness can make him realize that he must ask for other films. This is possible: Heaven is always ready to get other films for you. The only thing it will not do is change the screen, for it is just the right shape and size and perfectly well made. There is nothing wrong with the screen; it is the pictures that need to be changed.

Take the case of a criminal, a thief or murderer. His consciousness is constantly besieged and worried by fear of the police and the possibility of going to prison. He has set certain processes in motion and now they are reflected on his conscience,[1] robbing him of his peace of mind. The conscience of someone who has never done anything wrong, on the other hand, has no reason to be troubled by fears of any kind. The thing is obvious: when someone does something dishonest he loses his peace of mind because his consciousness receives worrying impressions

---

1 Conscience: that aspect and function of one's consciousness which pronounces judgment on the moral quality of one's actions and motives.

from all sides, and even if he tries to pacify it he
cannot do so because it does not depend on his
consciousness: as long as he does not change his
behaviour his conscience will never be at peace.
So you see how ignorant human beings are: they
never know on what level they have to act in order
to remedy the situation. Just try to quieten your
conscience and sleep peacefully again if you have
committed a crime! You cannot do it. You will
always be worrying, 'Someone must have seen
me. Someone suspects. They're coming to get
me!' You will never know a moment's peace
again, however hard you try. And that is how people make themselves ill.

All one's misdeeds result, sooner or later,
in physical or psychic illness. But it is quite
impossible to convince human beings of this!
They think they have control of every dimension
of themselves and can do whatever they please
with impunity, but the poor things soon find
out how little real power they have. If they
have done something wrong they will never
improve their psychic condition, however hard
they try. No one has ever succeeded in doing
so, yet: no one! However great a magus may
be, even if he commands the forces of nature
and is obeyed by the spirits, if he has the misfortune to do something wrong all his powers

will not save him. For, I assure you, there is
no power capable of soothing a troubled conscience, none!

You must rely neither on your powers nor on
your will, but only on your own straightforward,
honest, honourable conduct. If you do this you
will be saved: you will be free! But as soon as you
transgress a law all your powers are wiped out,
and they will only be restored if you make reparation. And it is precisely here that the difference
between a true magus and an ordinary man can
be seen: a magus takes care to repair his mistakes
immediately. This is where his power lies: in the
fact that he sets things straight at once. If he did
not do so, whatever the extent of his knowledge of
magic, it would still not be enough to calm his
conscience. But as soon as he makes reparation it
has an indirect effect on his conscience and peace
and calm reign once more.

It is necessary to talk about these truths at
length because they are unknown to most
thinkers. There have been so many false ideas
spread about human conscience that it is difficult
to convince human beings of the truth. A tormented conscience will never be permanently
healed by drugs or psychoanalysis. There is only
one sure cure and that is to make reparation.

II

Man's consciousness places him midway between the lower and the higher worlds and if he is not on his guard, if his consciousness is not fully awake, he is in danger from the dark forces of the lower world, particularly from those on the astral plane, which are constantly trying to get hold of him and to crush and devour him. This is why the Lord says, 'My son, give me your heart', because the very first place the Devil tries to get into is the heart. The heart corresponds to the astral plane and, as the astral plane is in contact with the physical plane, it is much more easily influenced by the dark forces of the underworld than the intellect or the soul or, above all, the spirit. However many evil things you do you can never drag the spirit down with you. The spirit is a spark which is too close to God ever to be extinguished or lose its brilliance. When, for example, one speaks of someone doing something in a 'spirit of revenge', in point of fact it is not his spirit that is involved at all. The spirit has no part in anything evil. But people do not know what the spirit is and often confuse it with the mind or intellect.

The Lord says, 'My son, give me your heart' and you reply, 'Why Lord? I've promised it to my sweetheart!' 'Yes, I understand that', replies the Lord; 'But give it to me all the same, because all your sufferings and misfortunes are caused by the fact that you keep your heart for yourself, and it is bound to get you into trouble.' So many people, even really exceptional people, have let themselves be led by their hearts into all kinds of follies and misdeeds! Oh, the heart! No one is proof against the demons bent on capturing the human heart. This is why you must seek heavenly protection by giving your hearts to God; if you do this God will send messengers of light to occupy your heart and guard it from every evil.

But if man has to take care not to let himself be seduced by the attractions of the lower world, he must also take care not to abandon himself utterly to those of the higher world. He has to work in collaboration with the beneficial forces from above, but without ever losing sight of the right balance between the two worlds. His life is on earth and he must not leave the earth before his time. If he severs his ties with the earth in order to reach Heaven sooner, he may, perhaps, dwell in the immensity of space and light, but he will fail in his mission which is to work on earth with the tools and methods of Heaven. Man's consciousness must be a consciousness of the centre, of the frontier between the world above and the world below.

A very old tradition depicts man with an angel of light on his right and a spirit of darkness on his left: this expresses exactly the same idea, that man is situated midway between the world above and the world below. The angel instructs him and gives him good advice, while the devil does all it can to lead him into error and claim him as its victim. One might well wonder why the angel and the devil do not fly at each other's throats directly and battle it out between them: the winner would take the prize, the wretched human being! But that is not how it happens: they treat each other with perfect respect. The devil does not try to harm the angel and the angel does not hurl lightning at the devil. The reason is simple: the angel and the devil are simply symbols of the two worlds, the world above and the world below, between which man is placed, and it is up to him to decide in which direction he wants to go.

You could take yet another image to describe the situation and say that that which is below and which is our constant temptation, is the moon, for the moon represents our instincts of greed and sexuality; whereas above us is the sun which represents our soul and spirit, God Himself. The idea is always the same: high and low, above and below, Heaven and Hell; and man, thanks to his faculty of consciousness, stands between the two and has the possibility of choosing to climb up to the heights or to let himself drop down into the abyss.

As human beings are composed of several different bodies, they actually have several different consciousnesses. In fact, on the physical level, each cell of a man's body possesses its own consciousness. Consciousness is not confined to the brain. Every cell of every living organism has its own consciousness, on a smaller scale, of course, but consciousness nevertheless! In fact at the very bottom of the scale, even rocks and stones and metals possess consciousness, but the difference here is that their consciousness does not dwell in them but very far away from them. Plants, too, have a consciousness which dwells at the centre of the earth: if we want to communicate with plants and get them to understand us and react, we have to get in touch with their consciousness in the centre of the earth. And animals have a consciousness which is collective, not personal; it exists outside the individual animals and each species has a group-soul to guide it. Man is the only one in whom consciousness dwells in each individual. For all the other realms of nature, consciousness remains outside the individuals. This is why animals, for instance, have fixed periods in which they mate, lay their eggs, migrate, moult and so on: they all obey the one group-soul. Only human beings, although they are still an integral part of the universe, have a Self, an individual consciousness, a personal will.

As I was saying, therefore, every cell of every organ has its own consciousness, and as the cells of the liver, spleen, lungs, etc., all have different functions and responsibilities, they all have different sorts of consciousness. However, as they are all connected to each other, exactly like the individual animals of any one species, they too have their representatives, their group-soul, which is in the brain. All the cells of the body have their representative in the brain whose responsibility it is to make their requests known and to express their satisfaction or their dissatisfaction. The pattern is exactly the same as that which applies on political and social levels: a group of citizens elects a member of Parliament or a group of workers delegates a member of their union to represent them and defend their interests. Yes, you see: it is exactly the same pattern. Human beings cannot invent anything which does not already exist in some part of their own body or in the universe as a whole. Through intuition or memory, or by persistent groping, they inevitably arrive at the laws and phenomena already created by Cosmic Intelligence.

In the front of the brain are cells which are the conscious representatives of the whole body. The other cells of the brain are also representatives, but on the unconscious or subconscious level. Self-consciousness is situated in a small number of cells in the front of the brain, and all the rest corresponds to the subconscious. For example, the cerebellum which lies at the back of the brain, is the seat of sexuality, and the cells of the cerebellum also have their representatives which go and clamour for their rights before the central forum. Men and women often experience certain needs without being aware of the fact, and this is the reason why they are sometimes very astonished by some of the dreams they have at night. Dreams are nature's way of bringing to our attention certain needs and aspirations which have remained buried in the depths of our subconscious. Consciousness, as I have already said, is a screen or bulletin board on which we can read the wishes and demands of the different 'selves' which go to make up our twofold nature, the higher and the lower.

A human being is a combination of his two natures and the screen on which they project their images. He can act indirectly on the screen of his consciousness, therefore, by acting on one or other of his two natures. At the same time, his actions can have repercussions throughout the length and breadth of the universe, in both Heaven and Hell. For a human being is something immense, his roots reach out to every part of the universe, and this is why it is so difficult, impossible in fact, for him to know himself. He manifests himself sometimes in one world and sometimes in the other, and it is the screen of his consciousness which gives him some idea of what he is doing. He can use this screen as a mirror in which to examine his features and get to know himself. He cannot act directly on this mirror, but he can act in every sphere of the universe thanks to his will, his imagination and his powers of thought, and the mirror simply shows him the reflection of his acts.

Man is a being who has worked for billions of years, to accumulate particles from every region of space and, thanks to these particles, he has managed to construct his physical, etheric, astral and mental bodies and even the first elements of his causal, buddhic and atmic bodies. And now he exists in all these different bodies and all these regions, and is in touch with powers and forces which are reflected in his consciousness. If he is intelligent and clear-minded he will observe this screen and decipher the images on it and be in a position to say, 'Aha, my thoughts or will or desires have stirred up the mud at the bottom of the swamp: I can see it on the screen.' In the same way, if he has stirred up something in Heaven he will see the splendour of it on his screen. This is how he learns; this is how he becomes conscious of reality; this is how he begins to realize that there are certain laws and that it is up to him to make up his mind to act with greater intelligence and wisdom, to be more careful and more reasonable so as to avoid projecting pictures of disorder and ugliness onto his screen. But all the images reflected on the screen of man's consciousness still do not reflect the sum total of his activities: his possibilities for action are far greater and, in fact, he cannot even know how far his actions reach. A man's consciousness reflects only one minute part of all that goes to make up his life.

A human being, therefore, lives in all the regions of space and is formed of particles coming from every one of these regions. This is why, whatever goes on inside you, you should always try to get a clear view of it and know where it comes from. You should be able to tell the origin of every desire, feeling or thought: whether they come from your lower or your higher nature; what colour and scent they have, and what entities correspond to them, for everything that exists fits into its own place in the scheme of things. So you have to get used to studying yourself like this, with the help of the mirror provided by your consciousness.

Man is host to a whole world. A man can give food and shelter to any number of secret enemies without knowing it until, one day, they suddenly declare themselves. They have been there for ages, no doubt, but he has never noticed them before, because they have never shown up on the screen of his consciousness. When they do come to light the individual falls ill, either physically or psychologically. Or, on the other hand, he has perhaps been giving hospitality to angels without realizing it and then, one fine day, they appear in his consciousness and he is amazed to find that they had been with him for a long time, helping and sustaining him.

A human being is something immense, but he does not know himself. In his higher, divine Self, he knows himself of course, but he has to get to know himself here, through the work of the brain, as he exists materially, and it is this that is so difficult. I am sure you have already watched a kitten playing with its tail: to begin with it does not know what it is, so it gets quite a shock when

it bites it ! But you are very like that kitten yourself : one day you discover the tip of a tail and, not
knowing what it is, you give it a good bite, then, of
course, you let out a howl because you have suddenly and painfully discovered that that tail
which seemed to have a life of its own is a part of
yourself.

A human being is scattered throughout
space, but he is going to have to find himself one
day, and our 'tail' is our physical body, and it is
through the physical body that we have to get to
know ourselves, through our material reality.
This is why our lives are so complicated and
difficult, because we often collide with other people or things without in the least realizing that
they, too, are ourselves. This truth is the foundation of all ethics. If we have been told that we
must not injure our neighbour it is because, in
doing so, we would be injuring ourselves. Our
true being is everywhere, in everything, so that it
is we, ourselves, who are the first to suffer if we
inflict pain on others. And the same is true for
joys, of course. Morality is based on the
knowledge that a human being fills the whole of
creation. So now you see why you always have to
take care to do good, because the first to benefit
from the good you do is yourself — the self that is
present in your neighbour !

As I have said, every single thing that exists possesses some form of consciousness and, depending on its level of evolution, that consciousness is more or less distant from the physical body. The distance between the physical reality and consciousness is greatest in the mineral realm; this is why minerals are in a state of inertia. With plants, and even more so with animals, consciousness is closer to the physical being. And, the consciousness of a human being dwells within him, and this is why he is a thinking being.

But man has to go beyond this. As I have already said, if you cultivate wisdom and light you will develop your causal body which will become one with your mental body. If you cultivate pure, absolutely selfless love you will develop your buddhic body which will become one with your astral body. And if you cultivate your inner strength and do all in your power to accomplish God's will, you will develop your atmic body which represents the primordial power, and it will become one with your physical body. The personality and the individuality, therefore, will become one, and then man will be all-powerful on the physical plane, all-loving in his heart and all-knowing in his intellect. You have to understand that that which is below is like that which is above, but in reverse: if this were not so nothing would make any sense. The body which is at the top in the higher Self is not in direct contact with the one at the top in the lower self, but with the one at the bottom. For the time being they are apart, separated from each other by that screen on which both of them project their image. But one day, when they have become one, the screen will no longer be there, or rather, everything will be one vast screen, for one cannot know everything and be everywhere with one small screen. If you are limited you have a small, limited screen, but if you know no limits any more, the whole universe becomes a screen and you are everywhere, you know everything.

12

THE SUBCONSCIOUS

Ever since the first years of this century, the subconscious has been a popular subject of study and discussion. Unfortunately, psychoanalysts who set out to explore this region of man's inner being have no idea of the dangers, of all the pre-historic monsters lurking there: dinosaurs, bron-tosaurs, diplodocuses, and many more besides. Yes, all these creatures still exist. They disap-peared from the face of the earth a long, long time ago, but they still live in man in the form of instincts, feelings and desires. The fact that their physical bodies have disappeared does not mean that their astral bodies are no longer on earth. By no means! In fact, not only the monsters of prehistoric times, but all animals are present in man's subconscious through the medium of their astral bodies. This is why, when psychoanalysts who have no knowledge of Initiatic Science launch into a reckless exploration of a person's subconscious on the pretext of getting at the root of his problems, they start stirring up the subterranean layers in which these animals are sleeping, with the result that they wake from their sleep and pounce on the person to devour him.

Now, I am not saying that you have to ignore the subconscious completely: not at all! In fact I have given you methods that you can use in order to make it contribute to your spiritual work. You have to know, for example, that any veritable transformation has to be accomplished not by the power of conscious thought, but by the powers of the subconscious. This is why, if you want to see your spiritual aspirations brought to fruition, you have to learn to plant their image in your subconscious. If you work on the purely conscious level you will eventually realize your dreams, but it will take much longer than if you have learned to work with the subconscious, for it is the subconscious which has the greatest power over matter.

What does the subconscious correspond to? You will remember that when I spoke to you about the different levels of consciousness, I explained that they corresponded to the different provinces of nature: the unconscious corresponds to minerals, the subconscious to plant life, consciousness to animals, self-consciousness to human beings, and superconsciousness to the great Masters and Initiates. The subconscious, which is linked to the vegetable kingdom, is very close to the physical world, far closer than the superconscious. And this is why, if you manage to plant your hopes and desires in the region of the subconscious they will come about much more rapidly. This is the principle involved in hypnosis: when you hypnotize someone you act on his subconscious and he does whatever you tell him to do without hesitation, whereas if you gave him the same instructions when he was awake and fully conscious, he would almost certainly not obey so promptly!

This means that there are methods you can use in order to hasten the realization of your aspirations. You will get results more rapidly on the spiritual level if you concentrate and meditate on the goal you want to achieve just before going to sleep, for then the powers of your subconscious will lend you a helping hand. Personally, I have used this method, for years, and if I have accomplished a little more than many others it is precisely because I have worked in this way.

Most human beings are content to brandish ideas. Oh, of course, I do admit that many of their ideas are strokes of genius. They are sublime! But ideas have to become facts, and there are many ways in which this can be done. I have just mentioned one of these ways, but one can also try to convert ideas into concrete reality by improving the way one lives and by accomplishing each detail of one's daily life more perfectly. We must learn to eat, breathe, walk, sleep and so on, more perfectly, for all these acts are closely associated with our subconscious life, and if we know how to perform them correctly they can contribute to bringing divine ideas down into material reality. And while we are on the subject of sleep, if I have insisted so often on the importance of your state of mind just before you go to sleep, it is because sleep helps to crystallize that state of mind in your subconscious. So you must always go to sleep with the best possible thoughts and desires in mind for, in this way, you contribute to their realization.

There is no lack of methods for a disciple who undertakes a sincere effort to transform himself. I have often told you that whatever we do is recorded within us: each of us has his own private record library. If someone returns, even after a very long time, to a place in which he had experienced a great love, he will be overwhelmed by memories and emotions of the same kind. The sensations experienced in the past are less intense no doubt, but they are still there. Similarly, if someone returns to the place in which he had been persecuted, beaten or tortured, he too will be seized by the same emotions of horror and fear that he experienced in the past. All this proves that these impressions have been recorded in the subconscious and that, given the right conditions, they can be brought to the surface again.

And now, if you really want to transform yourself you can attempt to recall the most beautiful moments of your life and immerse yourself in them once again. You have certainly all lived through sublime moments when you were lifted out of yourselves by a whirlwind of inspiration and light. Get out your records of those marvellous moments and listen to them, by which I mean, reconstruct the same conditions in your minds so as to experience the same effects again. You will very quickly begin to feel the same emotions and repeat almost exactly what you lived through before, and you can do this just as often as you like. In future, therefore, when you experience a moment of light and divine bliss, remember that it is all being recorded in your subconscious and that you will be able to get it out, one day, and relive it all over again.

So, you see, there are innocuous ways of working with the subconscious, but beware of psychoanalysis: even if you are in a state of deep anxiety and depression I do not advise you to undergo psychoanalysis. There are probably a few psychiatrists who have managed to heal some of their patients, but they often do not know exactly how or why, and in many cases they have done more harm than good. There are better ways of healing psychic disorders than by delving into the depths of the subconscious, rummaging about amongst the relics of the past and arousing the dinosaurs !

And yet there is one thing we must recognize, and that is that, however ineptly it may be applied at the moment, the craze for psychoanalysis is a sign that the time has come for man to explore the dark, unknown depths of his own being. At the moment he is only just beginning : he is groping his way about without really understanding how these regions are organized and structured, how all the different elements and materials hang together or what powers and entities are at work in them. In spite of the fact that they have none of this information to start with, a certain number of researchers, doctors especially, have launched into an exploration of the subconscious, urged on not only by their own audacity, but also by certain forces abroad in the world today, the forces of the Aquarian age. And although the means at their disposal are very limited, they have already gleaned a few scraps of truth and this is proof enough that the time has come for us to descend into this other aspect of creation and to get to know it.

The subconscious is a vast and very dangerous region, comparable to the depths of the ocean. If you try to go down into it without the necessary equipment, you will come to a bad end, for it is full of monsters waiting to devour you. Everyone knows that deep sea divers and speleologists need special equipment when they go down to great depths. In fact, any dangerous undertaking requires not only appropriate physical training but also special protective equipment. And yet, when it is a question of going down into the deep recesses of their own nature, people imagine that it is easy, that they are in no danger. The truth is that the greatest dangers lie in these regions and you must be properly equipped. The question now arises: how does one find the right equipment?

It is not as easy as all that. The psychic equipment you need can only be found in the region of the superconscious, above the level of consciousness and self-consciousness. You have to be sure to do some serious work in this region before you can safely dive down into the subconscious. This means that you not only have to learn a certain number of things about the structure of these subterranean regions and the entities that live in them, but you also have to develop certain virtues and qualities, particularly purity and self-mastery, so as to have the protection of a brilliant aura as you descend into the abyss. But most psychoanalysts know nothing about these different regions of the subconscious, some of which are, literally, Hell. They are inadequately trained and they do not know that, like divers in the past who used the old-fashioned diving suits, they have to maintain a link with the surface, a rope by means of which their team-mates can pull them up in case of danger. Nothing in their way of life distinguishes them from the common herd; they make no attempt to purify or strengthen themselves spiritually, and yet they plunge into deep waters dragging others down with them.

Of course, if that is your idea of sport, you are always free to go and match your strength against that of monsters and evil spirits, but I warn you in advance that if you do so, relying only on your own resources, you will be soundly thrashed, devoured and annihilated. Before you venture into those regions you must ally yourself to the higher spirits of the world of light, and ask them for arms and protection; once you have done that you can go off to battle, for when they see that you are well armed, the spirits of darkness will flee before you. And as the heavenly entities who have befriended you know very well that man has to explore his own depths before he can complete his evolution, if you do find yourself in danger they will not abandon you.

But whatever happens, don't let yourself be swayed by the fact that psychoanalysis is fashionable, and start dabbling rashly in the quagmires of the subconscious.

13

THE HIGHER SELF

I

Very often, when I have been travelling overnight in a train, and all the other passengers were fast asleep, I have opened a window and looked up ahead towards the locomotive, thinking that the engine driver was up there in the dark, his eyes shining out of a face blackened with coal dust, watching over the well-being of all those passengers who were sleeping so peacefully. The thought of that poor fellow all alone up there, and who was not allowed to sleep because he was responsible for the safety of his passengers, used to make a great impression on me.

This image of the train can perhaps help you to understand a very important point concerning the inner life. There is another kind of train whose engine driver is not allowed to go to sleep, and that train is each one of us. Our body, our cells can go to sleep, but our higher Self never sleeps. It is always awake and vigilant, directing and guiding us. At least, this is the case for an Initiate or an enlightened disciple, but most human beings are so estranged from their higher Self that it is as though everyone on the train were asleep, both the passengers and the engine driver.

We always have to keep one part of ourselves awake. In fact, before we go to sleep at night we should remember to put ourselves in the care of that inner Watcher who guards us while we are fast asleep. Jesus told his disciples to 'Watch and pray', and many Christians have thought that he meant that they should actually stay awake at night. In their eagerness to be faithful to this precept — although they understood it wrongly — they would get up in the middle of the night to pray and meditate. The result was that they exhausted themselves by struggling against their need for sleep and ended by destroying the natural rhythms of their bodies. But the vigilance Jesus was speaking about was on a higher level. To keep watch on the physical level is not the most important: we have to carry our vigilance up to a much higher level and, while our physical body, our cells, are asleep and resting, keep watch up above, that is, we have to go and join the Watcher who never sleeps and share in his vigil.

And where shall we find this eternal Watcher? You can find him in his home in the centre of the forehead between the eyebrows. This is why he sees and records and understands everything that goes on. He is completely motionless and impassive and you must try to join him up there. Yes, if you manage to keep vigil with him and to ask for what you want from that centre, your spiritual eyes will be opened, making it possible for you to explore the invisible world; when your body is sleeping you will be free to visit and communicate with the greatest and most marvellous realities.

II

The descent of the Holy Spirit is a symbol which can be found, in various forms, in all religious traditions, but more often than not it is not properly understood. You must not think that the Holy Spirit is an extraneous entity, foreign to man. No, the Holy Spirit is man's higher Self, the most luminous, powerful, divine peak of man's being. Perhaps you will ask, 'Well, since so many people have received the Holy Spirit, does this mean that there are as many "Holy Spirits" as there are individuals?' No: there is only one divine, cosmic Holy Spirit, and each man's higher Self, being divine in nature, receives its spark from this one Spirit and becomes like Him. When a man receives the Holy Spirit it is his own spirit that descends into him, his own spirit which is none other than his higher Self who dwells in the sun.

Every human being is linked to his higher Self which is only waiting for the day when it will be possible to enter and take possession of him, for it is man who, by reason of all his impurities, puts obstacles in the way. If, one day, a man really manages to purify himself and reach true holiness, the Holy Spirit will descend into him and he will be capable of doing marvellous deeds. But the Holy Spirit does not split Himself up: He is the cosmic Spirit, the one Godhead. And our higher Self, too, is of the same nature: it is made of the same quintessence, the same light. It is a spark in the one great Fire, a drop in the one cosmic Ocean.

Take some quicksilver, pour it out onto a clean surface and you will see it split up into a multitude of minute drops. Now, if you push all the drops up against each other you will see them come together and blend into one again. But if you try the same experiment on a dusty surface, the droplets of quicksilver will not come together again. And within us we see the same phenomenon: the layers of impurities in us prevent the Universal Soul, our own soul, from blending into one with us.

You can understand, now, why it is so tremendously important to purify oneself: because without purity the union between our higher and our lower Self cannot take place. And as long as this union has not been effected our higher Self remains aloof and apart from us; it has its own powers, its own knowledge, its own tremendous resources, but it can do nothing for us. It is perfect, omniscient and all-powerful, part of God Himself, and yet it can do nothing to help us.

Yes, this is one of the most difficult things to grasp: that there exists within us a being who can see everything, who knows everything and who can do everything and who, nevertheless, remains motionless and impassive whatever we do. Suppose that you do something wrong: since you are in contact with that other part of yourself which is on high, why did he let you do it? Why does he let us go on making blunders and creating situations which work against his interests? He knows very well that we are going to go astray, that we are going to cause ourselves suffering and come to regret our errors, and yet he never intervenes in any way. And in fact, is it not possible that it is our higher Self which actually pushes us into those errors? Yes, there is a great mystery here! While we are down here, weeping and wailing and 'stewing in our own juice', our higher Self is up there in untold bliss, oblivious to our suffering. And when we talk to him about our good intentions and hopes, why does he do nothing to bring them about? We are not separate from him and yet, when we are suffering he remains coldly indifferent and leaves us to our sorry plight! Obviously, we are going to have to learn how to touch his heart!

Our higher Self lives in a region beyond what we can properly term our being; beyond our physical, etheric, astral and mental bodies, even beyond our causal, buddhic and atmic bodies because, although these are made of extremely subtle materials, they are, nevertheless, bodies and, therefore, material in essence. Our higher Self is not a body; it manifests itself through the medium of our bodies but it belongs to the region known to cabbalists as Ain Soph Aur: Limitless Light.

Our higher Self has the power to do anything. The whole problem is to get it to use that power: we have no idea how to persuade it to want what we want it to want — and therein lies our tragedy! What can we do to kindle the good will of this entity? He is so far away from us and yet we represent, however inadequately, a tiny fraction of himself.

Our earthly self is made up of so many changeable, unreliable, contradictory 'selves'! And since it is we who are responsible for these unruly 'selves', it is we who have to suffer and make reparation for them. Our true Self, the Self whom we have to seek out and get to know so as to become one with it, never commits a crime or strays from the truth: it dwells permanently on high in the realm of light and purity, and it is up to us to work hard so as to be able to rise to the same level and become one with it. But in the meantime, here on earth, there is something known as 'I' which serves as a kind of 'visiting card' for all the other 'selves' which live at the same address; all those weird and wonderful 'selves' who are so utterly unlike each other: a poet, a miser, a cook, a lier! But I myself: who am I? We don't know. The self that we know is a fictitious being who includes all the others and is punished or rewarded for their crimes or good deeds. One of our 'selves' filches something from a neighbour, whereupon another, honest 'self' who sees this, is shocked and disappointed: he cannot understand how such a thing could happen!

Once we really make up our minds to know and unite with our higher Self, he hears about it and it makes him very happy. Whatever else we do leaves him utterly cold and indifferent. If you become a general, a minister, or an emperor, if you are hurt in an accident or living in the depths of poverty and despair, it is all the same to him. The only way to arouse his interest is to let him see that you really intend to get to know him, that is: to get to know yourself. Then he will begin to pay attention to you, and all the weakness, obscurity and pain that have afflicted you will fade away, because other forces begin to take effect. There is a parallel between this process of becoming one's true Self and the phenomenon that causes a caterpillar to metamorphose into a butterfly. The caterpillar shuts itself up in its cocoon and, shortly afterwards, a beautiful, light, brightly coloured being floats away from the husk: the caterpillar has become a butterfly!

Nature has placed signs everywhere for the purpose of teaching disciples and helping them to understand the kind of transformations they must produce in themselves. Human beings delude themselves into thinking they are magnificent creatures. In fact, though, they are like caterpillars: so clumsy, unsightly and destructive, robbing the trees and bushes of their leaves and creating havoc wherever they go. But as soon as they decide to turn inwards, to reflect and meditate and renounce certain base impulses, they trigger new forces within them, and before long a light and lovely butterfly flutters out as free as air, to feed no longer on leaves but on the nectar of flowers. The butterfly is a symbol of the soul which has escaped all bonds and restrictions and this is resurrection: true resurrection. You must not think that the resurrection spoken of in the Bible is a resurrection of the physical body: there is no resurrection of the physical body. There is only an awakening of the spiritual element in that body which had been asleep and which is now ready to burst into full bloom.

There are various methods we can use in order to develop our higher Self, and one of them consists in concentrating on our ego, our human self. This self is very limited and even illusory, that is true; but it is a reality all the same. Even if we say that it does not exist, it still exists as inexistence! The first method, therefore, consists in using this frail medium, this screen of the self, one's consciousness, which is not you and yet is yourself, part of you, a very remote manifestation of the higher You. Start by holding on to that consciousness; cling to it, do nothing else, only that: be conscious, and remain like that for several minutes, just holding on to the consciousness of your self. And as your consciousness down here, on earth, is linked to your superconscious above, in your higher Self, after a few minutes of attention and concentration you will gradually touch your higher Self.

Then there is another method that you can use if you want the qualities and virtues of your higher Self to be infused into your lower self, and for this you have to use your imagination. You are sitting there, thinking about your Self high up above, and you imagine that he is looking down at you; that You are looking down at yourself, seeing yourself in the difficult, imperfect circumstances of life on earth. With this thought in your mind, you keep the current flowing between your lower self down below, and your higher Self up above. In this way you restore the link, the true link which binds you to each other: down here you are thinking of your Self up above, and up above you feel the contact with the self below who is conscious of the Self above!

It is very difficult to explain this: you are both one and two. You are two because you are up above and down below, both at the same time, but the consciousness that you have of that duality makes you one. You can close your eyes and be clearly conscious both of yourself, down here in your room, a living, thinking being, and of that higher Self up above, who possesses all powers and all knowledge and who is reflected in you, who sees himself in you. He sees himself and smiles — and laughs! And you? You look at him from down here and see what he is like, and he sees you, too. And then the two poles of your being, the lower and the higher, begin to come together and, one day, they actually fuse into one; your lower self no longer exists; that lower self which was only a reflection, disappears and only your real Self, your higher Self remains.

And all discouragement, weakness and darkness disappear also and you become omniscient, immortal and eternal!

You have to imagine not only that your higher Self is watching you but also that he knows that he is watching himself as he exists through you, through your brain, and that he recognizes the bond between you. The contact established by this mutual recognition awakens your superconsciousness because, since your whole being is reflected on the screen of your consciousness, your higher Self is included, however faintly, in that reflection, and it is this reflection of your higher Self which enables you to establish a bond with him. This reflection may be a very fragile little thing but its quintessence is the quintessence of Heaven itself: even if it is only a reflection of yourself it is still part of you. Even a person's reflection in a mirror is made of the fluids and forces left by that person. Even your shadow on the ground is a reality. In fact sorcerers in Africa use the fluidic traces left by a person's shadow when they want to cast a magic spell on him. People think that a shadow is not a reality, but it is: it is made of one's fluidic emanations. Why are some dogs able to find people by following the scent of the fluids emanating from them? Suppose, therefore, that a disciple is capable of 'following the scent' left by his higher Self on the screen of his consciousness: in this case he will end by finding and joining him on high. Little by little his consciousness expands and grows to take in the whole universe, he feels himself to be the Cosmic Being, he bathes in eternity.

I can give you yet another exercise: it consists in concentrating all your attention on the back of the head, on the occiput. Try it for a few minutes and you will see that something begins to happen, your whole body begins to vibrate and you will feel as though sparks were running through you. But be sure not to do this for too long at a time: you must stop as soon as you feel as though you had touched a nerve centre which creates a tension and vibration in your whole body. When you first practise this exercise you must be extremely careful not to go on too long.

Hindu mystics have given us a formula which is as profound as it is simple: 'I am He.' This means, 'I do not exist as a separate, independent entity. It is thanks to Him that I exist, but only as a reflection. If I want to find myself I must find Him, He who created me. I am non-existence, illusion; He is the only reality.' God penetrates every aspect and dimension of the universe which He Himself created, and nothing in creation can exist apart from God. To seek God, therefore, is to seek oneself: the work is the same and it is a work that lasts a very long time. From time to time you suddenly feel yourself overflowing with light; without warning you find yourself thrust upwards into the superconscious and dazzled by the immensity and the beauty of that world. But, unfortunately, these moments never last very long and, once again, you drop back into the daily grind with the same old worries and weaknesses to contend with, feeling cut off from the Godhead and your own higher Self, a detached morsel, forgotten and unwanted. But when this happens, don't just sit there: make an effort to get the current flowing again between you and your higher Self. If you persist, patiently and sincerely, you will have that feeling of being cut off less and less frequently until, one fine day the light will always be with you; you will have gone over to the other side of the river, you will be safe, once and for all.

I am sure that, now, you understand better the inscription carved over the door of the Delphic Oracle: 'Know Thyself'. True Initiatic knowledge is to fuse, to become one in an act of love, as the Bible tells us that 'Adam knew Eve', or 'Abraham knew Sarah'. True knowledge is a melting into one, so when the Initiates said, 'Know thyself', they were saying that man is not who he thinks he is and that he must get to know who he really is. To know oneself is to identify and fuse into one with one's true Self, the higher Self who dwells above in the region of the spirit. That is why we have to cast off everything which constitutes only our outer wrappings, our rags and illusions, and rise higher and higher until we become one with our own spirit, our higher Self.

The whole meaning of Initiation, I repeat, is to teach man to detach himself from his lower nature so as to vibrate in unison with his spirit which is his true Self. When he manages to do this, then he possesses all the qualities and attributes of the spirit: power, mastery and knowledge. To become one with one's higher Self is to become one with God. Yes: to find oneself, to know oneself, is to melt into oneness with the Godhead, for the spirit which lives in man is never separated from God. When he seeks himself, when he finds himself, man reaches the supreme consciousness of living and breathing in God.

Editor-Distributor

Editions PROSVETA S.A. – B.P. 12 – 83601 Fréjus Cedex. FRANCE

Distributors

AUSTRIA
HELMUTH FELDER VERLAG
Kranebitteralle 88/144 – Posfach 33
A – 6027 Innsbruck

BELGIUM
VANDER S.A.
Av. des Volontaires 321
B - 1150 Bruxelles
PROSVETA BENELUX
Van Putlei 105 B-2548 Lint

BRITISH ISLES
PROSVETA Ltd.
The Doves Nest
Duddleswell Uckfield,
East Sussex T N 22 3 JJ
Trade orders to:
ELEMENTS Books Ltd
Unit 25 Longmead Shaftesbury
Dorset SP 7 8PL

CANADA
PROSVETA Inc.
1565 Montée Masson
Duvernay est, Laval, Que. H7E 4P2

GERMANY
URANIA Steinsdorfst. 14
D 8000 München 22

HOLLAND
PROSVETA BENELUX
M' Laan
Zeestraat 50
NL – 2042 LC Zandvoort

HONG KONG
HELIOS
31 New Kap Bin Long Village
Sai Kung N.T., Hong Kong

IRELAND
PROSVETA IRL.
84 Irishtown – Clonmel

ITALY
PROSVETA ITALIE
19-2 Via Ennio 20137 Milano

LUXEMBOURG
PROSVETA BENELUX
Van Putlei 105 B-2548 Lint

NORWAY
PROSVETA NORGE
Postboks 5101
1501 Moss

PORTUGAL
PUBLICAÇÕES
EUROPA-AMERICA Ltd
Est Lisboa-Sintra KM 14
2726 Mem Martins Codex

SPAIN
EDICOMUNICACION, S.A.
C/ de las Torres 75-77
08033 Barcelona

SWITZERLAND
PROSVETA Société Coopérative
CH - 1801 Les Monts-de-Corsier

UNITED STATES
PROSVETA U.S.A.
P.O. Box 49614
Los Angeles, California 90049

**PRINTED IN FRANCE
JULY 1987
EDITIONS PROSVETA, FRÉJUS**

— N° d'impression : 1505 —
Dépôt légal : Juillet 1987
Printed in France